This book is writt

And dedicat
John, Micah, Daniel, Tabitha and Thomas
in the hope that my miscellaneous thoughts
may direct them to the perfect Father,
in whose image they have been created.

Miscellaneous Thoughts

As I Pass By.

Ian Cameron

ISBN-13: 978-1514886595

ISBN-10: 1514886596

Table of Contents

Foreword

These all died in faith, not having
received the things promised, but
having seen them and greeted them
from afar, and having acknowledged
that they were strangers and exiles
on the earth. (Hebrews 11:13)

This Bible verse intrigued me for years. I don't know when I first realised that I was a 'stranger' on earth. It may have been when I went to Argentina to teach English as a second language. I certainly felt like a foreigner and stranger there. If it wasn't in Argentina (I was in my late twenties then) it must have been some time soon after. But I wonder if I would have realised I was just passing through, just a 'stranger and an exile' if I'd not read about Abraham's experience. It's a good thing to learn, while you're still relatively young, that we're just passing through, and I thank God that he revealed this insight to me when he did. I also thank him for making known to me how I (and anyone else) can have eternal life, because if this life were all there is, the ultimate futility of it would be sadness and frustration indeed.

As I've passed by, I've noticed common thinking and themes among the people I've met, whether Christian or not, and when I started to read the Bible more regularly and thoughtfully in my early thirties, I began to see and understand that the Lord had a lot more to say about work, death, money etcetera than I realised. Most of the thoughts included here have come from a sermon series I preached in 2014 and 2015, called 'The Christian Life - its helps, its hindrances, its hopes, and its fears.' The subjects mentioned in this volume shape our lives in some form or another, and they all help us, or hinder us, to live for God's glory as the days tick away.

Anyone who follows Jesus Christ will find that He is the light of life (just as he promised) and by following him, he will not stumble in the darkness. For the true light, which gives light to everyone, has come into the world, and can be clearly seen by anyone who wishes to see it. I hope that the following pages will help others walk in the light of Christ a little more clearly. If my thoughts do not achieve that, I know the fault will lie either with me, (or perhaps with the reader) but not with the Light itself - for He is perfect in every respect.

I.W.C, Paignton, 2015

On Work...

Jesus answered them, "My Father is working until now, and I am working."

How does work help us, both as humans and, particularly, if we are Christians? It's good to remember that God worked in the beginning and rested from his creative work. Work was given to Adam in the garden. And of course, Jesus said:

> "My food is to do the will of him who sent me and to accomplish his work." John 4:34

Work is inherently a good thing. God, who is all good and can do no wrong, worked and still works. The first Adam worked. The second Adam worked. Every man works, and those that don't feel unfulfilled. Work gives a sense of identity. It's the first thing a man does when he introduces himself, he tells you his occupation. Women work too, although generally women derive their identity from their husbands, and then from their children.

We ought not think that work at home is not work, just because its unpaid. In a way, work at home is paid. The deal for a married couple usually is, 'wife you work at home, and I will provide for you a free home and food all the rest of your days. We're a team, you work at home and help us raise the children, I'll work elsewhere.' Of course feminism has played nicely into the hands of men, because now many men expect their wives to work outside of the home, and to continue to do most of the house-work as well. But in any case, the point is — work is a good thing, in and of itself. When we work, whether it be cutting the grass or feeding our children, or cleaning dirt away or writing a newspaper article, we are mimicking God. Because God still works, he sustains all things and oversees all things. He removes sin and feeds and waters the earth.

In that sense work helps us become more like God. In the beginning God set Adam as ruler over the earth, to work it and keep it. However, not all work has equal value, and Jesus makes a distinction between regular work, work which will perish, and work which will have eternal value. We see this in John 6:27.

> "Do not work for the food that perishes, but for the food that endures to eternal life, which the Son of Man will give to you. For on him God the Father has set his seal." Then they said to him, "What must we do, to be doing the works of God?" Jesus answered them, "This is the work of God, that you believe in him whom he has sent." So they said to him, "Then what sign do you do, that we may see and believe you? What work do you perform? Our fathers ate the manna in the wilderness; as it is written, 'He gave them bread from heaven to eat.'" Jesus then said to them, "Truly, truly, I say to you, it was not Moses who gave you the bread from heaven, but my Father gives you the

true bread from heaven. For the bread of God is he who comes down from heaven and gives life to the world." They said to him, "Sir, give us this bread always."

Jesus said to them, "I am the bread of life; whoever comes to me shall not hunger, and whoever believes in me shall never thirst. But I said to you that you have seen me and yet do not believe. All that the Father gives me will come to me, and whoever comes to me I will never cast out. For I have come down from heaven, not to do my own will but the will of him who sent me. And this is the will of him who sent me, that I should lose nothing of all that he has given me, but raise it up on the last day. For this is the will of my Father, that everyone who looks on the Son and believes in him should have eternal life, and I will raise him up on the last day.

Now what is God's will with respect to work? Jesus tells us in verse 29.

"This is the work of God, that you believe in him whom he has sent."

That's the work God wants us to do. But why? Why does God want us to believe in his son? Why does he want us to do this work? The answer is in verse 40.

> For this is the will of my Father, that everyone who looks on the Son and believes in him should have eternal life, and I will raise him up on the last day.

All work we do in this life will perish. The British empire, a big project, has perished. The work on my father's farm has perished, inasmuch as the livestock have long since gone to market, and the farm has been sold to somebody else. Nothing we do here has an eternal perspective, except it be founded on God's work. For it's his will that those who believe in his son should live forever.

Thomas Arnold, the Headmaster at Rugby, used to say that a Christian education is one where the student is taught God's will for his life, and a non-Christian education is one where the student is not taught God's will, or if he is taught it, he is given no help to do it. So an educator's work, if he wants it to have lasting value, is not to teach just maths or MacBeth, but more importantly, to teach his student to look to the Son of God and believe in him.

A wise perspective on work:

Genesis starts with the account of God's creative activity. Every aspect of our world is the work of his fingers and God celebrated what he had made: 'It is good.' As we work we reflect the image of our worker God. Work was given as a gift to Adam and Eve before the fall (Genesis 2:15). It was a good gift and so it is right that we gain satisfaction from our work. Yet our work will end. Death is a given to us all and so it is wise to develop an eternal perspective, desiring to leave a legacy for others: 'For a person may labour with wisdom, knowledge and skill, and then they must leave all they own to another who has not toiled for it' (Ecclesiastes 2:1).

This leads us into the second part of how work impacts the Christian life, namely how it hinders us. The first part is that work helps us by making us be a little like God, who is creative and made work to be part of the created world. Mankind is to tend the earth and the creatures in it. Work in this life is temporary, but there is a work, that is believing in Jesus as our Lord and Saviour, that leads to eternal life. Work gives us a sense of purpose and identity, but we all know that what we work for will not last, because we will not last. And so we come to consider how work hinders us in the Christian life.

Its obvious that in many ways work hinders us from enjoying life. The Bible explains why this is so.
Because you have listened to the voice of your wife
and have eaten of the tree of which I commanded you,
'You shall not eat of it,'
cursed is the ground because of you;
in pain you shall eat of it all the days of your life;
thorns and thistles it shall bring forth for you;
and you shall eat the plants of the field.
By the sweat of your face you shall eat bread,
till you return to the ground, for out of it you were taken;

for you are dust, and to dust you shall return.
Genesis 3:17-19

Here God is speaking to the first man about the consequences of the first sin. Adam listened to his wife, instead of God's warning, and he decided to find out for himself what good and evil are. As a result evil entered into the world, because you cannot know what evil is like, until you have experienced it. And this is why we have difficulties in the workplace. The ground is cursed, the very place we work will bring forth thistles and thorns, troubles which have to be removed. So in the classroom the thistles may be unruly students, or simply lazy students, who don't do their homework. In the office it could be the secretary who does not do her work on time or in a good way. Alternatively, it could be the over-bearing boss. On the farm it really is weeds and insects that eat the crop or plague the animals.

The point is that work is now cursed. Where, in the beginning work was fun and easy, now it was hard for Adam and Eve. By the sweat of his brow Adam had to work, and ultimately he would return to the dust that he came from.

And so it is with our workplaces. At home the mother cleans, but the hoovering still needs to be done the next week. At the office the manager sorts out one problem, but another comes along. Even in the church, where we would expect there to be fewer problems because Christians don't go out of their way to sin, there will still be problems and thistles and thorns. These may be caused by the cares of life, or just insensitivity on the Christian's part, or indeed on the minister's part. In this life there will be troubles. It is unavoidable, because we live in a fallen world where people most people neither listen to God's son, nor obey him.

And so work hinders us from enjoying life, because we find problems there. We find people who are rude and annoying, we find people who take one end of stick and refuse to acknowledge they are in error. Sometimes we are those people, sometimes they come across our path. Consequently, work can be a real struggle.

But God allows all these things to happen for a reason. And one of those reasons is that each thorn we come across reminds us that this world is fallen. If you look for happiness in the work place, you will never find it perfectly there. We will have good days, we will have bad days. We will have times of highs and then real lows when we want to chuck it in and take up new employment. But the problem will be the same in the new place. This world is fallen. What is remarkable about the account in Genesis is that there was a time when work and this world wasn't fallen. There was a time when sin and selfishness did not exist, and all was peaceful and in harmony.

Non-christians often complain about suffering in this world. 'How could a loving God allow it?' they say. It strikes me that suffering is the very thing a loving God would send, and allow to happen, that people might wake up and recognise that this world isn't perfect, (and we're often the cause of it). I was getting my hair-cut once and the barber asked how much I wanted taken off. I said, 'please give me a short hair-cut, maybe a number two. I'm getting tired of seeing all this grey hair in the mirror.' And he replied, 'if you're getting tired of looking at this grey hair, you know what the solution is, don't you?' I said 'no, what's that?' He said 'don't look in the mirror.'

Well, it got me thinking. Why does our hair go grey as we get older? (It's not just having children that does it.) God allows it so that we may know that we are getting older, and that our time here is coming to an end, that we might turn to him and make peace with him, turning from sin and asking for our sin to be forgiven, and being reconciled to God.

So work hinders us from being perfect people because of sin. This is why it can be hard to get out of bed on Monday morning. But the toil and the trouble in the workplace is not without its purpose. It is to remind us that we no longer see God face to face, like Adam did, that we have often chosen for ourselves to live disobediently to God, not in obedience to him. And it will only be in the world to come, which will be peopled by citizens of God's kingdom, that perfect peace and happiness will be found. It won't be found in this life. There will be work there, but it won't cause us difficulties like it does here.

Let me mention another way in which work can hinder us as Christians. Its easy to think that the work we do is important, and we can become so busy doing our duty, that we neglect those other duties which God has given. Perhaps things like devotion to our families, the support of our aged parents or young children. Time spent with other Christians, maybe at church on a Sunday, maybe in a Bible study group. We can get so busy with work that the very thing which seems our help, is unto us an occasion of falling. Work can become an idol. This is a hindrance to the Christian, I think.

So work does hinder us now, as well as help us. And what I've described so far is, I think an accurate assessment of work for most of us. Thus we come to hopes. What is the hope God has with respect to work? If you're a Christian, what or how is it that God wants us to approach the work he has given us?

As God's beloved children we model a different way of working, bringing glory to our Father through our good deeds. Jesus says 'Let your light shine before others, so that they may see your good works and give glory to your Father who is in heaven.' (Matthew 5:16). Christians are told that our true 'boss' is Jesus. Paul recognised that he was a servant of Jesus, that Jesus was his 'boss.' (Romans 1:1) It was not because he was an apostle but because he was a Christian that Paul came to see Jesus as his boss. Christians must do the same, and in so doing, see that God expects that we should serve our bosses wholeheartedly, as if we are serving the Lord:

> Slaves [employees], be obedient to those who are your masters according to the flesh, with fear and trembling, in the sincerity of your heart, as to Christ; not

by way of eye-service, as men-pleasers, but as slaves of Christ, doing the will of God from the heart. With good will render service, as to the Lord, and not to men, knowing that whatever good thing each one does, this he will receive back from the Lord, whether slave or free. (Ephesians 5:5-7 - NASB)

Our workplaces will be transformed if we see it as the place where we serve the Lord. Whether it's customers at the counter, clients in the law office, children in the playground or at home. With good will we must render service, as to the Lord, not unto men.

Furthermore, our work is the main way in which God provides us with the necessities of life. Paul states that 'If a person will not work, he shall not eat' (2 Thessalonians 3:10). In addition, our work enables us to be generous towards those who are unable to provide for themselves. Finally, although our work may be characterised by the effects of the Fall, we are urged to 'Be joyful always; pray continually; give thanks in all circumstances, for this is God's will for you in Christ Jesus' (1 Thessalonians 5:16-18).

So God has hopes for us, in our work, if I can put it that way. And if we believe the Bible to be true, as I do, having rejected evolution years ago and come to having a full confidence in God's word, then we can have every hope that our work and our workplace, will be part of our lives which is transformed by our following Jesus Christ.

And so finally we come to fears. For the Christian Life has its helps, its hindrances, its hopes, its fears. I don't know if you've seen the movie 'Shadowlands', starring Anthony Hopkins as C.S. Lewis. Throughout the movie Lewis is shown in banter and friendship at the local pub with his brother and other Oxford dons. You probably know that he was an Oxford professor for 30 years. Yet in one very telling scene, Lewis is sitting alone in the library with another don not far from him. And he says to his friend:

'Don't you ever feel a terrible sense of waste?'

And his friend looks up from what he is doing, and with no banter but complete seriousness says, 'of course.'

And that, ladies and gentlemen, is a great fear for many on this planet, certainly it is the fear of anyone who for a moment, stops and thinks — hang on, what is life all about? Why am I here day after day, year after year, doing the same old thing? In all our work, there is a fear of waste. That we are just wasting our time. That all that we are doing is ultimately pointless. This is the cry so elegantly phrased throughout the book of Ecclesiastes.

> What has a man from all the toil and
> striving of heart with which he toils
> beneath the sun? For all his days are full
> of sorrow, and his work is a vexation.
> Even in the night his heart does not rest.

This also is vanity… Vanity, vanity, all is vanity. (Ecclesiastes 2:22-23)

Many of us have this deep-seated fear that all we have done, will in fact, be a complete waste of time. That either we will lose it all, or after we've died, someone else will mess it up. We have a fear that our work, and our lives, will have somehow been wasted. Is there anybody who can say to us 'well done good and faithful servant. Enter into the joy of your master'?

Well, the good news of Jesus Christ is that there is such a person. It is the Lord himself. In several places he speaks of work. In one place he tells a parable of three servants who had received talents from their master. Their master went away for a long time, but when he came back he called them each to give an account. Two of them had used their talents well, but one had hidden his talent, and that one was resoundingly criticised by the master. Why was this so? What was the lesson of the parable?

The lesson is this. We are all given talents of some form or another. Some people have greater talents than others, but no talent is wasted if it is used for the Master's glory. But every talent is wasted if it is buried and not used for Him. He gave us our talents, lets use them, whatever they may be, in the work place. If we do that, if we use our talents for serving God, wherever our workplace may be, then we can be sure we will hear our Lord say 'well done good and faithful servant — enter into the joy of your master.'

We don't have to fear our lives being a waste, if we live them for him. Hear the words of a man who for many years was not a Christian, and then became one.

> But whatever gain I had, I counted as loss for the sake of Christ. Indeed, I count everything as loss because of the surpassing worth of knowing Christ Jesus my Lord. For his sake I have suffered the loss of all things and count them as rubbish, in order that I may gain Christ and be found in him, not having a righteousness of my own that comes from the law, but that which comes through faith in Christ, the righteousness from God that depends on faith— that I may know him and the power of his resurrection, and may share his sufferings, becoming like him in his death, that by any means possible I may attain the resurrection from the dead.

The apostle Paul says that no matter how successful he may have been before knowing Christ, it is nothing compared to knowing him afterward. He says that real life is not found in success at work, but in knowing Christ and being in him, having a righteousness, that is a right way of living that comes from having faith in him. We need not fear that our work is wasted if we live and work for Jesus Christ. So let us listen to him as he says to us.

> We must work the works of him who sent me while it is day; night is coming, when no one can work.

If we do our duty in work and see it as God's work — that is, not our work only, nor the devil's work, but actually God's work. That we see being a mother, lets say, or helping in the garden as God's work, in which we are busied. If we see ourselves as fellow-workers with God, then what is more natural but to ask his aid and his blessing on it?

Let us come to Him and do so. But there seems some unwillingness to do this. We will talk about our jobs, and think about them — but do we pray about them? If we take our work and think it to be ours and not God's, then the work is no longer being sanctified, and perhaps we dread to speak to God about it, knowing that in his sight we have rendered both our work and ourselves sinful. It would be a very good thing for us to do, to bring our work, as it were, every morning before God, and ask for his aid and blessing on it. Then, at the end of the day, we would do well to look over our work and ask God to pardon us where we have failed. And he will, for he is gracious and merciful. But in this way we, that is, Christians, can learn to see our work as God's work.

Finally, let us not fear how long our works may last, but consider how soon we must leave them.

The shortness of our own time bids us remember that we are but God's instruments, appointed to labour for a little while on a particular little part of His great work; but that neither its beginning nor its finishing belongs to us, nor can we so much as understand the vastness of its range. Our best praise is that bestowed on David, that we serve our own generation by the will of God, and then fall asleep, and be gathered to our fathers, and see corruption. Whether our work may endure on earth or no, we can never tell; the wisdom of the wise, and the virtue of the good, have too often remained without fruit, except that eternal fruit which remains for all those who work God's work heartily, without presuming to think that it is their own.

We do not have to fear our work will be meaningless, if we see that it is God's kingdom that will last, and join ourselves to building that up, and working at our jobs in such a way that others see our good work, and know that we are diligent and hard-working because of Jesus Christ - working for him, and not just our pay cheques.

So some applications as we close this chapter:

1) Lets pray about our work and bring it to God, especially at the start of the day, but also at its close.

2) Lets pray for those who are in authority over us at work. Remember Paul says 'first of all, then, I urge that supplications, prayers, intercessions, and thanksgivings be made for all people, for kings and all who are in high positions, that we may lead a peaceful and quiet life, godly and dignified in every way. This is

good, and it is pleasing in the sight of God our Saviour'.
(1 Timothy 2:2)

3) Lets ask God for the wisdom and skill to do our work well (Exodus 35:35)

4) Lets apply ourselves to our work: 'One who is slack in his work is brother to one who destroys' (Proverbs 18:9)

5) Lets learn from others who are wiser and more experienced: 'Wisdom is found in those who take advice' (Proverbs 13:10); and accepting feedback (Proverbs 5:11)

6) Lets recognise that our lives do not consist in the abundance of our possessions — and God's son himself calls us a fool if we think they do. A Christian works for his master, not his possessions.

The Christian life, its helps, its hindrances, its hopes and fears…

Work:

Helps us be like God.

Hinders us from time spent with others and is a place where sin is present.

Hopes that we will believe in God's son, serve him and transform our place of work.

Brings a fear that our work will be meaningless.

On Money... (Part I)

"No one can serve two masters, for either he will hate the one and love the other, or he will be devoted to the one and despise the other. You cannot serve God and money."

Money has been used for many good things and for doing great good. The Lord Jesus was supported by the wealth of women (Luke 8:2). But while money can certainly be used for good as well as for evil, often it is the source of much evil. For many years I thought that money was essentially a neutral substance, with the rightness or wrongness of money depending entirely on how we use it. But in latter years I have started to think that there may be something intrinsically deceptive about money. Jesus says we cannot worship God and mammon. He even calls money, unrighteous (see Luke 16:9, 11). Historically the Bible shows that:

- For money Aiken brought disaster on the Israelites.

- For money Delilah betrayed Samson.

- For money Elisha's servant became a leper.

- For money Ananias and Sapphira lied, and were struck dead.

- For money Judas betrayed the son of Man, and was ruined eternally.

Money is a product of our fallen world, where things are not as they were in the beginning, nor as they will be when Jesus returns. In the beginning, our ancestors didn't need to labour for food, there was work for them to do but not in order for them to eat. There were no shop-keepers, they owned everything and ate directly from what the trees provided. Similarly, at the end of time, we're told money will no longer be needed (Rev 21:6, 22:17).

> "Come, everyone who thirsts,
> come to the waters;
> and he who has no money,
> come, buy and eat!
> Come, buy wine and milk
> without money and without price." (Isaiah 55:1)

So money is a product of a fallen world. Some things in this life we can expect to see in the next one. Clothes, trees, lions and lambs. But we won't have money — what would we need it for?

However, for the moment we're stuck with it. How does money help us? Well, its more convenient to keep money in your wallet than walk around with eggs to barter. A lot of money can give a sense of security. From a Christian perspective, money provides us with a foil against which we can stand for Christ. For invariably temptation comes from wealth. Moses, stood against the wealth of Egypt, because he considered reproach for Christ to be of greater worth. So in an unexpected way money can help us be better Christians because if we know that making a certain decision for Christ may hurt us financially, then probably that is the decision to make. For instance, if your boss told you to commit abortions and you knew that disobeying your boss meant you'd lose your job, money in this case helps you see what it means to be a disciple. A Christian would have to walk from the job, rather than murder an unborn child.

How does money hinder us? We're clearly warned that the love of money causes people to wander from the faith. It focuses our attention on the here and now. The love of money is a root of all kinds of evils. It is through this craving that some have wandered away from the faith and pierced themselves with many pangs. (1 Tim 6:10) We can hoard money, where the silent enemies of rust and thieves break in (James 5).

Money gives a false sense of security. If you think you've got money saved up, what happens if there's an earthquake? Or the bank collapses (which it will, at some point)? The sense of security that money gives can make us think our security and our peace comes from our money instead of from God. The Bible says, "Teach those who are rich in this world not to be proud and not to trust in their money, which is so unreliable. Their trust should be in God, who richly gives us all we need for our enjoyment. Tell them to use their money to do good. They should be rich in good works and generous to those in need, always being ready to share with others. By doing this they will be storing up their treasure as a good foundation for the future so that they may experience true life." (1 Timothy 6:17-19)

What are God's hopes and expectations of our money?

The Bible tells us that the Lord expects:

First, that we provide for our families. For if anyone does not provide for his relatives, and especially for members of his household, he has denied the faith and is worse than an unbeliever. (I Timothy 5:8) Second, that we pay our workers, tradesmen and employees on time. 'Come now, you rich, weep and howl for the miseries that are coming upon you. Your riches have rotted and your garments are moth-eaten. Your gold and silver have corroded, and their corrosion will be evidence against you and will eat your flesh like fire. You have laid up treasure in the last days. Behold, the wages of the labourers who mowed your fields, which you kept back by fraud, are crying out against you, and the cries of the harvesters have reached the ears of the Lord of hosts. You have lived on the earth in luxury and in self-indulgence. You have fattened your hearts in a day of slaughter. You have condemned and murdered the righteous person. He does not resist you.' (James 5:1-6).

Third, that we give generously and lend freely. 'It is well with the man who deals generously and lends; who conducts his affairs with justice.' (Ps 112:5). Fourth, that we recognise every good thing comes from God. Our money does not come from our jobs, it comes from God. 'As for the rich in this present age, charge them not to be haughty, nor to set their hopes on the uncertainty of riches, but on God, who richly provides us with everything to enjoy. They are to do good, to be rich in good works, to be generous and ready to share, thus storing up treasure for themselves as a good foundation for the future, so that they may take hold of that which is truly life.' (1 Tim 6:17-19.)

Fifth, that we pray for our daily bread, not trusting our pension pots or our salaries. 'Give us this day our daily bread, and forgive us our debts, as we also have forgiven our debtors.' (Matthew 6:11-12) Sixth, that our hearts will be soft so as to help the poor, and seventh, to use our money to glorify God. 'While Jesus was at Bethany in the house of Simon the leper, as he was reclining at table, a woman came with an alabaster flask of ointment of pure nard, very costly, and she broke the flask and poured it over his head. There were some who said to themselves indignantly, "Why was the ointment wasted like that? For this ointment could have been sold for more than three hundred denarii and given to the poor." And they scolded her. But Jesus said, "Leave her alone. Why do you trouble her? She has done a beautiful thing to me. For you always have the poor with you, and whenever you want, you can do good for them. But you will not always have me. She has done what she could; she has anointed my body beforehand for burial. And truly, I say to you, wherever the gospel is proclaimed in the whole world, what she has done will be told in memory of her.' (Mark 14:3-8)

What fears does money bring?

It seems to me that we, people in the West, (who in reality have a considerable amount of money), have a lurking fear that we might lose it. But the truth is that we will lose it at death anyway! 'There is nothing better for a person than that he should eat and drink and find enjoyment in his toil. This also, I saw, is from the hand of God, for apart from him who can eat or who can have enjoyment? For to the one who pleases him God has given wisdom and knowledge and joy, but to the sinner he has given the business of gathering and collecting, only to give to one who pleases God. This also is vanity and a striving after wind.' Ecclesiastes 3:24-26.

I've also observed that money is exceedingly strange. If you have none you don't fear financial loss. Westerners are prone to anxiety about money that non-westerners aren't, and I think its at least in part because we don't thank God enough for his generosity nor have faith that his generosity will continue.

From a Christian's perspective, we may fear we have not used our money wisely or sufficiently for God's glory (see the parable of the talents - Matthew 25:14-30). And can we truly say we have we learnt to be content in all circumstances?

Consider, if you're a parent, how much your son (or daughter) means to you? If he were kidnapped, wouldn't you pay all you can to have him safely released? Or, if your child was struck down with a deadly illness, wouldn't you give up all you had in order for him to be made well? If we, as parents know how much our children mean to us, how much more did Jesus mean to his Heavenly Father? And if God loved him this much, how much then, must we mean to him?

If we call on him as Father who judges impartially according to each one's deeds, lets conduct ourselves with fear throughout the time of our exile, knowing that we were ransomed from the futile ways inherited from our forefathers, not with perishable things such as silver or gold, but with the precious blood of Christ, like that of a lamb without blemish or spot. He was foreknown before the foundation of the world but was made manifest in the last times for the sake of us who through him are believers in God, who raised him from the dead and gave him glory, so that our faith and hope are in God. (1 Peter 1:13-22)

On Money... (Part II)

In the previous chapter I observed that money is a product of the fallen world, that before sin entered the world there was no money, and it appears that in the age to come there will be no money either, for there will be no need for it.

We saw the Bible outlines some of God's hopes and expectations for our money. Namely to:
- provide for our families
- pay our workers (tradesmen etc)
- give generously and lend
- recognise every good thing comes from him
- glorify Jesus and help the poor when we want to.

In this chapter we'll think a little more broadly about the question of stewardship. Stewardship is managing God's resources for the glory of God. All we have is only loaned to us by God, and Jesus taught that if we are faithful in a little, then God will entrust us with a lot. But we must beware lest we say in our hearts, 'My power and the might of my hand have gotten me this wealth.' We are told to remember the Lord our God, 'for it is he who gives you power to get wealth, that he may confirm his covenant that he swore to your fathers, as it is this day. And if you forget the Lord your God and go after other gods and serve them and worship them, I solemnly warn you today that you shall surely perish. Like the nations that the Lord makes to perish before you, so shall you perish, because you would not obey the voice of the Lord your God.' (Deuteronomy 8:17-20)

There appear to be six ways in which we can use our wealth.

- Spend it (perfectly legitimate).
- Give it away.
- Lend it (investments).
- Save it (set it aside for a specific purpose)
- Hoard it (stock-pile it with no planned use for it)
- Lose it, through theft or being fraudulently deceived or through a bad loan.

Those six things again.

We can spend money, give it away, lend it, save it, hoard it or lose it.

The thing to remember is that God has made mankind his managers, all the wealth we have, whether it be great or small, is to be used wisely for God's glory. Just as we read in the parable of the talents, not everybody gets the same amount, one gets more, one get less to start with, but all of us are expected to use our money for God's glory. Indeed, the Bible says …

Honour the Lord with your wealth
and with the first-fruits of all your produce;
then your barns will be filled with plenty,
and your vats will be bursting with wine. (Proverbs 3:9)

So lets consider those six points more closely.

One way we can use the resources God has given us is by spending our money. This is perfectly legitimate.

Because one of the Ten Commandments is 'Thou shalt not steal' we can conclude that it must be ok to have personal property, for if nothing is owned privately, then it cannot be stolen, as it belongs to everyone. In the New Testament we see Peter affirming this principle by telling Ananias and Sapphira 'your property was yours, to use as you wanted.' (Acts 5)

But we are warned against loving the things of this world. 'Do not love the world or the things in the world. If anyone loves the world, the love of the Father is not in him. For all that is in the world - the desires of the flesh and the desires of the eyes and pride of life - is not from the Father but is from the world. And the world is passing away along with its desires, but whoever does the will of God abides forever.' (1 John 2:15-17)

The Lord does not expect us to be guilty about spending money, but he also tells us that a man's life is not measured by the abundance of his possessions. Our consciences should start to afflict us if we spend too much money on ourselves. I heard a story about the Methodist preacher, John Wesley, being severely convicted because he bought a nice picture to adorn a room in his house. He had just got the picture up, and was going out, when he met the maid, who was shivering from the cold, whose old coat had worn out. Wesley rebuked himself sharply, not so much for spending the money on the picture, but for spending it when his servant was not properly clothed. We are free to spend money, but we are commanded not to love the things of the world, the desires of the flesh or of the eyes or of life.

Because there is something seriously heartless about us, if, in spending all our money on ourselves, we fail to see the needs of others.

Therefore, as stewards of the living God <u>we can give money away</u>. The Lord loves a cheerful giver, and Jesus taught it is more blessed to give than to receive. There is a great joy in giving, and there are many worthy charities, projects and people which we can give money to. Christians are urged in scripture to do good to all men, particularly the household of faith. It may be that we can give generously to family members, or friends directly, in some way. Its worth noting that the older we become, generally the richer we are, (because we've accumulated various gifts and inheritances, debts have been paid off and so on). This is why grandparents can often be more generous than parents. Giving away money, or gifts, may be a way in which Jesus' disciples can, and should, glorify God.

Next we come to <u>lending</u>, or investments. It seems to me all investments are essentially loans in different guises. I lend somebody, or a company, or a bank, my money with a view to getting some kind of return. I may call it an investment but essentially it's a loan I'm giving. A Christian will invest in things which are morally sound and socially useful. I can't see, for instance, how a Christian could lend money to a builder of a casino or a brothel.

But latterly I have been struck by two things I had not noticed before on the subject of lending. One I learnt a teaching from the Bible, the other is connected to it from personal experience. The teaching from the Bible is this. God's people in the Old Testament were commanded not to lend out money at interest. Look with me at Psalm 15.1, 5.

> O Lord, who shall sojourn in your tent?
> Who shall dwell on your holy hill…
> [the man] ***who does not put out his money at interest***
> and does not take a bribe against the innocent.
> He who does these things shall never be moved.

Notice that the man who does not lend at interest is one who is commended. And this is not an isolated case.

> "You shall not charge interest on loans to your brother, interest on money, interest on food, interest on anything that is lent for interest. You may charge a foreigner interest, but you may not charge your brother interest, that the Lord your God may bless you in all that you undertake in the land that you are entering to take possession of it." (Deuteronomy 23:19-20)

God's people were not to lend to one another at interest. To a foreigner they could, presumably to cover the risk of lending to someone they did not know. In Nehemiah 5 we read of Nehemiah's great anger at the Jewish people because the rich were forcing the poor to mortgage their fields and houses and even their children, while he, Nehemiah was lending them grain to pay for their debts. And so the creditors said 'Let us leave off this interest we have been charging.' The point is, is that lending at interest is considered to be a wrong thing to do.

Now-a-days, those of us who live in western societies expect to get interest on money we loan to the bank. We grumble if interest rates are low, because there is no proper return on our savings. But is there a different way. If you have savings and are in a position to lend some to a family member, why not lend them your money at no interest? I suggest this to you because it is the way God instructed his people to operate in the Old Testament and there's nothing in the New Testament which suggests now we should charge our brothers and sisters interest on money loaned to them. I also recommend it to you because of my own personal experience. I have been the recipient of very generous loans, at 0% interest by certain family members. And that has been a great blessing to me because each year I have been saved about £5000 in interest payments. So, on the subject of lending, I would say Christians should lend money, if we can, for the glory of God, on the principles God has laid out in his word. As Jesus teaches us:

> "And if you do good to those who do good
> to you, what benefit is that to you? For
> even sinners do the same. And if you lend

to those from whom you expect to receive, what credit is that to you? Even sinners lend to sinners, to get back the same amount. But love your enemies, and do good, and ***lend, expecting nothing in return***, and your reward will be great, and you will be sons of the Most High, for he is kind to the ungrateful and the evil." (Luke 6:33-35)

This teaching has reshaped my whole approach to banking. I have looked on the internet to find out if there is such a thing as a Christian bank. And do you know, there are at least two overtly Christian banks that operate in the United Kingdom? How we invest, that is, lend our money, can be done for society's good and according to Godly principles, if we will look into these matters.

To recap, as God's stewards, we can spend our money, we can give it away, we can lend it, but we can also save it.

As we consider the Christian life and the role of money in it, the very central point to have in our minds is that it is God's money, which we are to manage for his glory. We cannot keep it, because it is not ours. Even if all we did with our money was store it in the bank, when we die, God will give it to someone else. Indeed, we're told this in Ecclesiastes 2:26

'For to the one who pleases him God has given wisdom and knowledge and joy, but to the sinner he has given the business of gathering and collecting, only to give to one who pleases God. This also is vanity and a striving after wind.'

In the parable of the rich fool Jesus alludes to the folly of hoarding things up. It's ok to save money, but it's not ok to hoard it. Therefore, its important we know the difference. We save for a specific purpose, and when we've saved enough to achieve that purpose, we should spend the money for the item we have saved. For instance, a parent may save for his child to go to university, but when the time comes, the whole point of saving that money was to spend it on the education, not to try and hold to it even longer, but to spend it. So the parent should cheerfully give it over, pay the university bills, rather than think, how can I hold on to this for longer?

Lets learn a lesson from the ant, when the ant stores up for the winter, she does so in order to eat the food in the winter, not to store it up forever. When my father cut hay in the summer on the farm, it was with a view to using it for fodder in the winter. That was wise, but it would have been foolish not to have distributed the hay in the winter. The point is that it is foolish to endlessly save and save for no particular purpose, because we have then stopped saving and started hoarding. That is the difference between hoarding and saving. The hoarder accumulates and accumulates his money, but never with the intention of spending it.

The saver saves and saves, but with a clear goal in mind. We must be very careful that we do not be like the man in the parable who buried his money in the ground. If you have money that's just lying around, and has been for years, I'd urge you to reflect on whether that money is being used for God's glory, and I'd urge you to consider whether you've stopped saving and actually started hoarding. The Lord will take your money from you at death, so why not use it for his glory now? We are stewards of all God has given us, and with what he has given us we can bless others, or fail to bless them. But it is clear that the Lord's will is that we should bless others.

Which brings us from saving and hoarding to losing money. We are only stewards of God's money, that is, temporary managers of it, and it is possible of course that we might transfer the money the Lord has entrusted to us to a swindler, or we might be robbed. One of the ways in which money goes from one party to another is through loss. It is bad stewardship to thoughtlessly use our money in such a way that it is deliberately lost, which is, for instance, the likely result of gambling. We also need to make sure that we ourselves are not inadvertently stealing from others and causing them loss.

Now as far as loss goes, there is legalised plunder and theft pure and simple. Taxation is legalised plunder, Her Majesty's government has the right to take our money and we have no recourse to getting it back. If I were to come to you on payday and stick a knife into you and say 'give me 20% of your pay packet', I would be branded a thief. And rightly so. But the government can legitimately take that money and not be stealing - and our Lord tells us as much when he says we must render unto Caesar what belongs to Caesar. Furthermore, Jesus showed the rightness of paying tax when he and Peter pay a tax through the capturing of a fish, even though Jesus did not, as the ruler of everything, strictly have to pay tax.

But there is a question here which all Christians should think on, and I put it before you for your consideration. If we are in receipt of a benefit or pension to which we are entitled, but do not really need, say for instance perhaps child benefit or a particular pension, if we are in receipt of such that is surplus to our needs, we would do well to consider whether we should surrender that benefit or pension. Because the government picks another man's pocket on our behalf. The government is plundering a worker's pocket so that we can receive a benefit or a pension. And if we do not really need that benefit or that pension, our surrendering it will led to a reduced welfare budget for the government, and perhaps eventually to reduced tax for that worker. Do we realise that if 100,000 middle class Christian[1] families gave up £30 child benefit per week, then the country would save £160 million per annum, which would be enough to pay

---

[1] Of course, this would be true of any household giving up its benefit or pension. But since only genuine Christians are likely to make this kind of selfless sacrifice, I make the appeal to Christian families.

for 7200 soldiers or 7200 more nurses each year. Just be aware of this. One way in which we lose money is through taxation. We cannot stop being taxed, but we might be able to help stop government expenditure by refusing entitlements we don't need.

And we may say to ourselves, well its ludicrous and crazy and a poor use of God's generosity to deny ourselves something we're entitled to, even if we do not need it. But I would just say, in response to that, that that was not the attitude of Nehemiah, who was the governor of Judea about the time of King Artaxerxes. Look with me at Nehemiah 5:14-19.

> Moreover, from the time that I was appointed to be their governor in the land of Judah, from the twentieth year to the thirty-second year of Artaxerxes the king, twelve years, neither I nor my brothers ate the food allowance of the governor. The former governors who were before me laid heavy burdens on the people and took from them for their daily ration forty shekels of silver. Even their servants lorded it over the people. But I did not do so, because of the fear of God. I also persevered in the work on this wall, and we acquired no land, and all my servants were gathered there for the work. Moreover, there were at my table 150 men, Jews and officials, besides those who came to us from the nations that were around us. Now what was prepared at my

expense for each day was one ox and six choice sheep and birds, and every ten days all kinds of wine in abundance. Yet for all this I did not demand the food allowance of the governor, because the service was too heavy on this people. Remember for my good, O my God, all that I have done for this people.

We do have an example in the Bible of a godly man turning down his entitlements, because he knew that if he took what he was entitled, it would add to the debt and poverty of his people. And that example, seems to me, to be a very noble one, and a guide for us, if we are entitled to something but do not strictly need it.

On my street I have a neighbour who worked for the civil service. I do not know his personal circumstances, I know that he and his wife were saddened that they could not have any children. But this man was given early redundancy from the civil service when he was 51, I think he's in his sixties now. Let us suppose that his civil service pension is a modest £100 a week, just £5200 per annum. If that's the case, then this country will need all the income-tax paid each year, from two private sector taxpayers, each earning £25,000, to pay my neighbour's civil service pension, let alone his state pension.

The point is this. We are stewards of the money God gives us, but we do need to consider what we use our money for, and where that money is coming from. It is not good to lose money, but it may be right to forfeit some income if by taking it another person is deprived. This was evidently Nehemiah's view. We live in a country which believes in entitlements, and so we tend to believe that too. But God does not say we are entitled to other people's money, rather he says a labourer deserves his wages. Let us then be thoughtful about all the resources that pass through our hands. We do not want to lose the resources God has given us, but we are not loving our neighbour if we are causing him loss. In the next chapter, I hope to consider ways in which we might legitimately gain money. But for now, the point is, that in the Christian life we are stewards, managers, of God's property. Any money we have, we are only holding onto it temporarily. The money we have we will either spend, give it away, lend, save, hoard or lose. These are all possibilities but they are not all equally legitimate.

Clearly one of the lessons Jesus tells us in this parable of the talents is that we must and should use our talents, our wealth, wisely for God's glory and the advancement of his kingdom. The worst thing we could do with the money God has given us is bury it in a hole. The second worst thing we could do is put it in the bank, but that alone would be far better than leaving it in a hole or throwing it in the sea. But let us seek to be like the servants who were commended, they were those who used their talents for their master's glory.   Our master has gone away on a long journey, but he's given all of us worldly goods for his glory. To some he has given more, others less, but he clearly expects us all to use _his_ worldly goods for _his_ glory and the betterment of society. Let us reflect then on how we might do that, so that on our Lord's return, we hear him say 'Well done good and faithful servant; you have been faithful over a little, I will set you over much.'

On Money... (Part III)

And Jesus, looking at him, loved him, and said to him, "You lack one thing:go, sell all that you have and give to the poor, and you will have treasure in heaven; and come, follow me." Disheartened by the saying, he went away sorrowful, for he had great possessions. (Mark 10)

In the first chapter about money I reflected on the fact that money is a product of the fallen world, that before sin entered the world there was no money, and it appears that in the age to come there will be no money either, for there will be no need for it. I also suggested God's hopes and expectations for our money. These include:

- provide for our families
- pay our workers (tradesmen etc)
- give generously and lend
- recognise every good thing comes from him
- glorify Jesus and help the poor when we want to.

In the second chapter we saw that as stewards and managers of all that God has given us, we can spend money, give it away, lend it as an investment, save it for a purpose, hoard it for no purpose, and lose it. The great Methodist preacher, John Wesley, preached a sermon in which he argued one should 'Gain all you can. Save all you can. Give all you can.'

In this chapter we'll consider some lessons from Jesus' conversation with the rich young ruler.

Firstly however, lets note that money does not give any indication about a man's moral status. Someone with much money may be a very godly person, but equally someone with money might be a very wicked person.

There are seven common ways in which people gain money. Some people gain by **stealing**, for instance, pilfering. But a Christian must never steal. First, stealing is stealing whether we've stolen a great or a small amount. Getting off a bus or a train without paying is stealing. If you did this 1,000 times over the course of your lifetime you could be considered the great train robber!

Second, stealing is stealing whether we take from an individual, or from a corporation, or from the state. A child taking black-board markers from school is stealing, and so is an employee who makes long distance phone calls using the company phone.

Third, stealing is stealing whether the person has a lot of money or not. We must watch out for this because sometimes we will steal and justify it by saying 'well, my boss has plenty of money anyway. So what does it matter if I take a few pens, or some stationary?' Just because someone is rich, or because we're taking something from a company as opposed to a person, does not mean we're not stealing. And a Christian must never steal.

Exploiting -

Exploiting shortage is wrong. We've all noticed that when oil prices go up, suddenly the price of petrol or diesel goes up. But when oil prices go down, it takes a long time for the prices to fall. And this feels wrong — because it is wrong! But we also must not exploit the weaknesses of men e.g. men's minds by pornography. If I were a shopkeeper and someone came in whom I knew was struggling with alcohol, I would be sinning to sell him wine or beer or liquor. The Bible clearly says that God has made wine to gladden the heart of men, and our Lord changed water into wine, something he would not have done if wine were inherently evil, but it is still wrong to exploit people because of a particular weakness. Drug-dealing would be the same for a Christian. How could a Christian exploit a fellow human being in this way? It hardly seems possible. Note that in the time of Nehemiah, the Jews were severely rebuked for exploiting their fellow citizens when they were in great need and severe poverty. (Nehemiah 5)

Gambling -

In 2010 it was estimated that six billion pounds was spent in gambling in the United Kingdom. Now to put this into perspective, the entire budget for the building of two new aircraft carriers for the Royal Navy is £6.2 billion. In other words, what this country spends on gambling each year could fund the building of two aircraft carriers each year.

But what is gambling?

Three things make a gamble. First, there is an artificial risk that wasn't there before (thus gambling differs from insurance); Second; gambling always seeks to gain at someone else's loss; Thirdly, gambling seeks to get something for nothing. In other words without giving goods or services in return.

How can a Christian love God and put his faith in chance and luck? How can I love my neighbour and try to get something out of his pocket without putting something back?

Borrowing

'Neither a borrower nor a lender be' says Shakespeare's Polonius in his tragedy *Hamlet*. 'Owe no man anything except a debt of love' says the apostle Paul. It's brilliant advice and a good way to live. The Bible consistently portrays being in debt as something to be avoided. 'The rich rules over the poor, and the borrower is the slave of the lender.' (Proverbs 22:7) Wherever possible, Christians are wiser to pay with cash.

But what about a mortgage? That is a regular contract with regular payments, so as long as you don't get behind in your payments, you are not in debt. In one sense we are simply paying rent to the bank, instead of to a landlord. But remember, the more you borrow the greater the chances that you will get into debt. Therefore I'd recommend avoiding using the credit card as much as you can, indeed, you may do well to cancel the card entirely (if you can).

Investing

Jesus did mention investing in his parable of the talents. However, we could invest in such a way that we are in fact gambling, if we speculate with an attempt to get something for nothing. A Christian will invest in things which are morally sound and socially useful, and one of the problems of a unit trust is you do not have direct control over where the investment goes. When Christians lend (which is what we do when we put savings in the bank) we ought to watch out for seeking out the best interest rate. The more I think about it, the better it is, in my opinion, to try and do our lending privately (to family members usually), remembering not to lend more than we can afford to lose, and ideally lending without charging interest. This seems economic suicide but it is in fact simply following the Lord Jesus' command to treat others as you would want to be treated yourself. And if you would want an interest-free loan, then give one away (if you are in a position to lend).

Inheritance

It's quite clear that inheriting money is a valid way to pass on money, but inheritances do cause family squabbles. As the old saying goes, where there's a will, there are lawyers. In my judgement it would be better to give away our money while we are alive. Since Jesus tells me its more blessed to give than to receive, what stops me from giving while I am alive? Am I fearful that if I give much (or all) of what I have to my children, that at that point the Lord will stop providing me with my daily bread? God gives good gifts to all men, how much more to his children? A good father will do the same, and parents are told to save up for their children (2 Cor 12:14).

Working

Jesus was a carpenter, Paul a tent-maker. I gather that in Greek and Roman society one's ambition was to get as much leisure as possible. Consequently people sought to gain enough money to employ a slave, so that they could rest and have someone else do the work. But the New Testament says 'if a man doesn't work, neither should he eat.' Although the apostle Paul accepted gifts from churches which he had previously founded, in Corinth, Ephesus and Thessalonica he worked as a tent-maker and kept his house in Rome at his own expense (see Acts 18:3; 20:33-34; 2 Thessalonians 3:7-12 and Acts 28:30-31)

The Bible is filled with teaching on money. We must be careful not to be covetous, because when we covet we're becoming idolators. Money is a means, not an end. A man who receives and gives will be healthy, but the one who receives and keeps will be unhealthy. Consider the Sea of Galilee which has water flowing in and out of it contrasted with the Dead Sea, which only has water flowing in.

Money represents what we can buy here and now. The rich young ruler's problem was that money was going to keep him from following Jesus. That's a problem for many, but it needn't be, if we consider Jesus' promise that all who give up everything in this life will gain it back at the next.

Godliness with contentment is great gain...

So lets turn our attention to the rich young man. This young man wanted life, true life, and he admitted he didn't have it. He knew he'd have to be given life, because he says 'what must I do to **inherit** eternal life.' He felt he had to do something and he knew that Jesus was the man to speak to receive life — in its fullness.

Jesus replies to him and tells us — we are not good, there's only one who is good, that is God. God gives to the poor, God distributes all his goods, since all things belong to him. Jesus effectively said 'why do you call me good? There's only one who's good, do you recognise him in me?'

What did the rich man lack? He lacked Jesus. 'You need me', says Jesus. There will be in every person's life something that separates him from Jesus. For this man, what separated him from having Jesus was riches. This man's problem was that his possessions meant more to him than following Jesus.

This is a problem for many: Our possessions mean more to us than following Jesus. Now, in the first century AD, following Jesus literally meant following. It meant walking along the road in the dust of your rabbi. If you were going to follow Jesus today, literally walking after him, what possessions could you take with you? If you had a nice computer, you'd have to leave that behind. You'd have to leave your TV behind. You'd have to leave your bed behind. And almost all your clothes. What are we willing to leave behind to follow Jesus?

Sadly this young man did not want eternal life more than his possessions. And if we would follow after Jesus we must love him more than we love what we own. Possessions are for here and now. Only Jesus Christ brings abundant life for this age and eternal life in the next.

This is a genuine problem for those with wealth, and that affected the disciples, because many of the disciples were middle-class and well off, just as we are today. James, John, Peter and Andrew owned a fishing business with at least two boats between them and with employees. So when Jesus said 'how difficult it is for the rich to enter the kingdom' they saw the implications for themselves, just as we do today.

Did Peter have to sell his boats and his house?

Do we have to sell our things in order to be a disciple?

Well, possibly yes, but probably no. Lets note that a number of disciples had property. The letter to Philemon shows us that Philemon had his own house, and slaves, equivalent to our having employees today. Philip, who was a deacon, in the book of Acts, had a house in which he lives with his four daughters.

So what does Jesus mean? He means that if we want eternal life, if we want life that is real and full, life in abundance, life in the kingdom after the resurrection, then we need him in our life. And something will come between us and him. It could be wealth (and for many it is) for others, it's a relationship, for others, it may be a career, or children ('unless you give me children Lord, I won't follow you' or 'unless you accept my children as yours, even though they don't acknowledge you as Lord, then I won't follow you.')

Jesus loved the rich young man, but he saw what his problem was. His possessions would stop him from following Jesus. And they did, thus the young man went away with his face downcast. Now if possessions aren't a problem for you, in the sense that they are not stopping you from following Jesus, what is stopping you from following him? He is the great King who invites all into his kingdom, but although many are called, few are chosen. If it's not possessions, then what stops you from following Jesus? Truth be told, it will probably be money and mammon which stops Christians in the West from following Jesus faithfully and truly. It could well be money which makes us worship the Lord with our lips and not with our heart.

Well, if possessions are what stop us from following Jesus, here are some principles that may help us overcome their hold on our life. Giving is the key.

Give cheerfully, for the Lord loves a cheerful giver.

Give gladly, willingly, cheerfully. Levitical offerings we no longer bring, but free-will offerings we do.

Give generously.

Give secretly — we're told when we give, don't let your right hand know what your left hand has given. So once we have given something we should forget about it. We should not give expecting something in return. If that's our attitude, we haven't given a gift, but a bribe.

Give proportionately — as the Lord prospers you, give.

Finally, and most importantly, have faith in Jesus, that when he says:

> 'Truly, I say to you, there is no one who has left house or brothers or sisters or mother or father or children or lands, for my sake and for the gospel, who will not receive a hundredfold now in this time, houses and brothers and sisters and mothers and children and lands, with persecutions, and in the age to come eternal life. But many who are first will be last, and the last first.' (Mark 10:29-31)

In short, Jesus is saying, 'Am I more important to you than anything you own? Am I first? For if I am not Lord of all then I am not Lord at all.'

We cannot worship God and mammon.

On Friends...

"This is my commandment, that you love one another as I have loved you. Greater love has no one than this, that someone lay down his life for his friends. You are my friends if you do what I command you. No longer do I call you servants, for the servant does not know what his master is doing; but I have called you friends, for all that I have heard from my Father I have made known to you."

- Jesus Christ speaking to his disciples the night he was betrayed.

Biblically, friends are the people we walk with, those whom we allow to shape our lives. Some friends will prove to be false friends, they walk with us but they do not truly love us. They are friends of the moment, friends whom we have because we happen to be in the same classroom, or office or department. Other friends however, will be true friends. They are people whom we like to be with because we share a common interest and a common love. So it is that people join gardening clubs, or railway societies or whatever. And in those clubs and societies we make friends, and as long as our interest lasts, then very often the friendships will too. But there will need to be something greater than just a common interest if the friendship is to be deep and lasting.

It's clear that God wants us to have friends, for if that weren't so, Jesus would not have had any. As the perfect man, he lived his life as an example for us, and he did have friends. Amongst the twelve it seems he was closest to James, John and Peter. And amongst those three, he was closest to John. But it follows by definition that a man who has friends must have non-friends. Because when someone says of you, or of me, we are friends, then it implies immediately there are some who are not our friends.

Looking in the Old Testament we see Job had friends, although they weren't much help to him. We read that David had friends, classically Jonathan. But its also clear that Saul was not his friend. So as we think on this subject of friendship, friendship with others and friendship with God, let me ask you a few questions.

First, who is your closest friend of the same sex as you?

Second, who would consider *you* to be a close and reliable friend? Are there people whom you could say confidently 'so and so would definitely name me as their friend.'

Third, would Jesus of Nazareth, God's Son, call you his friend? How do you know if you're a friend of Jesus?

In life the ability to make friends and be a friend is something that lifts us from above the animal realm and makes us a little like God. Animals do not have friends, playmates perhaps, but not of the same order as men and women. Friends get together to discuss poetry or how to bring good news to a village - animals do not do these things. As for angels, do they have friends? I simply don't know - I hope so, for their sake. Because having friends is a wonderful thing.

Certainly God has friends. We know he does for we are told that Abraham was the friend of God. Now I'll tell you this frankly, although I may sound like a billy-no-mates, I don't have many friends. And I don't think I'm alone in this. Men particularly, but perhaps women too, find it hard to find lasting friendships. A friendship has to be about something, and we so rarely find someone who thinks the same as we do.

This is what is so impressive about David's friendship with Jonathan. The friendship comprised a deep affection for one another, and there was loyalty, even when David had to flee to the wilderness, Jonathan remained his friend. Its worth noting that their friendship lasted beyond the grave, inasmuch as David sought to look after Jonathan's son long after Jonathan had died. I imagine that the starting point for their friendship was their common respect for one another as soldiers. That respect grew and grew. David, of course, married Jonathan's sister, so that later they became brothers-in-law. And I think their friendship was, no doubt, strengthened by the recognition by both men that Saul was being unreasonably tyrannical towards David.

This opposition of Saul leads us into the subject of hindrances and fears with respect to friendship. Every friendship presents some degree of problem to those in authority. Jonathan and David's friendship was perceived by Saul to be a threat. Jesus and his disciples were considered a threat by the religious authorities, as well as a possible threat to the Romans. Any church, as a collection of disciples of Jesus, might be considered a potential threat to the government. Because what becomes of the government's power if we raise our voices loud enough and say, 'there is another king, one called Jesus'?

Headmasters and teachers always keep a wary eye on friendships that are being formed in the school or classroom. Parents are often concerned about the friendships their children make. This is because the Bible clearly says 'Bad company ruins good morals.' And herein lies a valuable lesson for those of us who wish to walk in the ways of Jesus Christ. We are warned against making friendships with world.

> You adulterous people! Do you not know
> that friendship with the world is enmity
> with God? Therefore whoever wishes to be
> a friend of the world makes himself an
> enemy of God. (James 4:4)

Now this verse inevitably raises the question of what does it mean to be a friend of the world, and how is it that I could be a friend of the world and therefore an enemy of God? I take it that no thinking person would wish to be an enemy of God, because our future can only be one of darkness if God is our enemy. But is it possible that we might accidentally become enemies of God by not being friends of Jesus? Jesus' friends must be, by definition, friends of God, for Jesus says "If anyone loves me, he will keep my word, and my Father will love him, and we will come to him and make our home with him" (John 14:22).

The issue runs like this.

Am I a friend of God or a friend of the world? It depends on whether I am a friend of Jesus or not. If I am, then Jesus, my friend tells me he and his father will come to me and make their home with me. So then the question becomes, well how do I know I love Jesus? Because a man might say he loves his friend but secretly hate him. How do I know I love Jesus? The answer is by keeping his word, or put another way, obeying his commands. This is what Jesus himself teaches us.

You are my friends if you do what I command you.
(John 15:14.)

The world will hinder us in our friendships with Jesus. It will tempt us to disobey his commands. We will have to choose. I saw a tee-shirt once which was trying to be funny. It said this in the front: 'Don't worry, Jesus loves you.' On the back it said 'but everybody else thinks you are a jerk.' I saw that shirt and thought to myself, 'well, you know what, I'd much rather have Jesus love me and the whole world think I'm a jerk, than have the whole world love me and Jesus think I'm a jerk.'

The point I'm making is this. Friends are a blessing from God, but some friendships will take us away from Him. Some friendships may hinder us, such to the point that we will have to choose whether to keep the friendship or lose it. The Bible says 'the way of the wicked leads the righteous astray' and 'don't be deceived, bad company ruins good morals.'

Biblically we see this happen in the life of David's eldest son Amnon. Amnon loved Tamar and was sad that he could not marry her. We are told that Amnon had a friend, whose name was Jonadab, the son of Shimeah, David's brother. And this Jonadab was a very crafty man. Now because Amnon listened to his friend Jonadab, Tamar was raped and ultimately Amnon lost his life. A classic example of 'Bad company ruins good morals.'

Friendships are good things, but they can hinder us in the Christian life — it all depends on the nature and intent of the friend. In saying this I do not mean to say that its impossible to have friendships with non-Christians, but I do think that its impossible to go as deep in the friendship as you could if the person were a Christian. I have a friend who likes golf, I don't like it so much. No doubt our friendship would be deepened if I started to like golf. In the same way, our friendships with non-Christians can only be deepened if they become Christians, but the friendship itself could hinder us because we may be tempted to choose our friend's desires over our Lord's, because they do not prize him nor value him. So, as an application, it could be worthwhile reviewing your list of friends in your mind, and check to see if they are leading you closer to, or away from, the Lord.

But lets turn from hindrances to helps and hopes.

Friendship as a form of human love that is not jealous like the love a husband has for his wife. Friends are happy for other friends to join the circle. In this context then, we can be confident that Jesus wants *us* to have many friends, but ultimately they will need to be his friends too. If they are disciples of Jesus, they will be friends for eternal life and they will be friends we can trust. A good friend really helps in life, and the Bible gives us some terrific insights how to be a genuine friend. A good example of this can be found in Proverbs 27:5-10.

> Better is open rebuke than hidden love.
> Faithful are the wounds of a friend; profuse are the kisses of an enemy.
> One who is full loathes honey, but to one who is hungry everything bitter is sweet.
> Like a bird that strays from its nest is a man who strays from his home.
> Oil and perfume make the heart glad, and the sweetness of a friend comes from his earnest counsel.
> Do not forsake your friend and your father's friend, and do not go to your brother's house in the day of your calamity.

Here are some ways in which we can help our friends. Firstly, friends may need to rebuke each other some time. Usually this needs to be done in respect to how our friend has mistreated someone else. If, for example, a Christian friend of yours is bad-mouthing his mother or father, a good friend will rebuke him or her. A good friend will say 'you know what, you shouldn't speak of your mother like that. The Bible says "honour your mother and father" and when you speak of your mum or your dad like that, you are disobeying God, and it is ugly.' Because sin is always ugly. Now if your friend is a good friend, he or she will immediately see that your words, which may wound, are faithful words.

When I worked at a school in London I had a friend who's marriage was on the rocks. I did not know it was so, because I was very naive. He had left his wife in Preston, Lancashire to work in London. It wasn't until I saw him holding hands with another woman at a pub one evening that I suddenly realised his marriage was in trouble. I said nothing to him, but texted him later that night saying how sad I was to see his marriage in trouble. I rebuked him (gently, I think), but I was the only one of his colleagues and friends to make any comment.

Well, in the end his marriage did fail, and he remarried. But he has subsequently became a Christian and he is the only one of my former friends and colleagues at the school whom I ever hear from. Because in sending him that text I showed him that I cared about his marriage. It was a faithful wound from a friend.

Thus in terms of applications, open rebuke is needed sometimes from a friend. Almost always in connection with a third party. If we rebuke friends because we feel they have mistreated us, we will almost certainly lose the friend, because they will simply think we have sour grapes. But we may be able to rebuke them gently (if its necessary) in connection with a mutual acquaintance.

Secondly, a faithful friend will give earnest counsel. Who doesn't need advice in this world? We all do. A friend is someone who offers clear and thoughtful suggestions. Advice is always the way forward in friendships, because there is something in us that naturally rebells against impositions. I know a man whose son had got a girl pregnant. He told his son he must marry the girl or he'd be cut out of the will. He would have been better, I think, to have simply advised his son and left him to take or leave the advice. Friends give counsel, not threats. The apostle Paul gave advice to Philemon regarding his slave 'Accordingly, though I am bold enough in Christ to command you to do what is required, yet for love's sake I prefer to appeal to you— …. I appeal to you for my child, Onesimus, whose father I became in my imprisonment.' A father has the right to command his children, and a boss his employees, but friends should only give earnest counsel.

Finally, we must be loyal. David in one of his Psalms says a blameless man does not take up a reproach against his friend. And here, in Proverbs 27:10, we read

Do not forsake your friend and your father's friend,
and do not go to your brother's house in the day of your
calamity.

So the point to note is we must not forsake our friends nor the friend's of our father. Loyalty is what is called for. The Bible gives much practical instruction with respect to friendship. Sometimes we may need to point out a fault to a friend, because we are always blind to our own defects. We must give earnest counsel, we must be loyal.

But let us turn to the best friend we can possibly have. Proverbs 18:24 is key here, I think:

> A man of many companions may come to ruin, but there is a friend who sticks closer than a brother.

There is a friend who sticks closer than a brother, and that is Jesus Christ himself. If we are to have friendships which last then we must be his friend and he must call us friend. Because it is only in Christ Jesus that people can receive eternal life. To return to what I said earlier, if I join a particular club, maybe stamp collecting or reading books or a movie club, I can make friends there. But those friendships must terminate upon death. The only way I can have lasting friendships is if I live forever and if my friends do. And the only way that can happen is if I am a friend of Jesus Christ, and my friends are too. Listen to Jesus on the night he was betrayed.

> Greater love has no one than this, that someone lay down his life for his friends. You are my friends if you do what I command you. No longer do I call you servants, for the servant does not know what his master is

doing; but I have called you friends, for all that I have heard from my Father I have made known to you. You did not choose me, but I chose you and appointed you that you should go and bear fruit and that your fruit should abide, so that whatever you ask the Father in my name, he may give it to you. These things I command you, so that you will love one another.

What a wonderful thing it is to know that the king of the universe has said to mankind, 'you can be my friend.' He calls us to be his friends. But if we are to be his friends we must change. This is the lesson of the parable of the wedding feast. The King compels people to come in and he sees a man without wedding clothes. 'Friend, how did you get in here', he asked. The man is speechless, and the host throws him out. Why? Because he did not change.

So what is the change that transforms us from being an enemy of Jesus to his friend?

First - A friend of Jesus obeys Jesus' commands. What kind of friend would we be if we never did what our friend asked us. 'Could you pick up milk for me on the way home?' A friend would do that, a false friend wouldn't. 'Could you telephone before you come around?' A friend would do that, if we'd asked him to. A false friend would not. 'Could you give me a lift to the train station?' A friend would do that, if we'd asked him to. A false friend would not. And so Jesus says 'you are my friends if you do what I command you.'

Second, Jesus commands his friends not to fear men. A fool fears men (we call this peer pressure today), but a Christian fears God. If we fear men, and run from them, then we aren't Jesus' friends. Look with me at Luke 12:4,5.

> "I tell you, my friends, do not fear those who kill the body, and after that have nothing more that they can do. But I will warn you whom to fear: fear him who, after he has killed, has authority to cast into hell. Yes, I tell you, fear him."

Third, a friend will lay down his life for his friends. He will not avoid laying down his life. This, from a Christian perspective will mean giving up our life daily, carrying our cross. It means a life of serving others, and putting sin to death. For some it may mean persecution. Is there anybody here willing to lose friends, lose a job or go to jail for Jesus? Would we be Shadrach, Meshach and Abednego?

Would we be a friend of Jesus? Then let us start small. Determine what your principles are, and if your employer crosses them, or people ask you to cross them, stand up for Jesus and so 'no.' Those Bed and Breakfast owners who were targeted by certain anti-Christian groups have laid down their livelihoods for Jesus. The Lord will not forget them, not in this life nor the age to come. They have been loyal friends of Jesus Christ.

There's a lot that could be said about friendship, but we must draw stumps somewhere. Lets recap those applications again.

First, a friend of Jesus obeys his commands. We need to know what those commands are — but to get us started, one is that we should love one another.

Second, Jesus tells his friends not to fear man, those who can kill the body or take away our jobs. Rather we must fear God.

Third, we must lay down our lives for our friend. He laid down his life that we might be saved from sin and God's judgement. We all remember our friend's death at the communion table. The table is open to anybody who is a disciple of Jesus. If there are sins we've committed since last coming to the table, confess them to the Lord and take encouragement from the words 'If we confess our sins, God is faithful and just to forgive us our sins and to cleanse us from all unrighteousness.' The table is open to disciples, to those who recognise Jesus as Lord, to those who are obedient to him. No disciple is perfect in his or her obedience, but we will know in our own heart whether we recognise Jesus as our friend, or if we don't. If you're not yet a disciple of Jesus, simply pass the bread and the wine along, but say to yourself as it goes by 'not today, but one day, I too will eat with the Lord.'

Let me close this chapter with the words of Jesus:

Greater love has no one than this, that someone lay down his life for his friends. You are my friends if you do what I command you.

Lets seek to be such a friend of Jesus Christ, that he can say of us, to the angels - 'do you see so and so there, see what a good friend he is. He always does what I command.'

A prayer about friendship.

O Lord, thank you for calling us to be your disciples, to be your friends. I pray that we would be true friends of yours, obedient to you, and bearing fruit. Forgive us our many sins, for the sake of your son. We confess that we've not been your friend the way you have been ours, please forgive us where we have disobeyed you. May we Lord, be like Abraham, who was willing to give up his own son because you asked him. May we demonstrate that same obedience to you, being willing to give up anything which hinders us from being faithful to you in every way. Bless our friendships, that they may be characterised by love and loyalty, may we be the best friends you could possibly have, and may we present you to others as the best friend we have.

In Jesus' name, Amen.

On Death...

The last enemy to be destroyed is death. (I Corinthians 15:26)

It may seem a little strange to share some thoughts about death, but a man must face his enemies square on. The truth is, death is the one enemy we cannot defeat. We know that our lives are like clockwork trains that have been wound up, and we simply do not know at what point the internal mechanisms will stop working, we do not know at what point we'll breathe our last. And the Bible pulls no punches with respect to death. It calls it exactly what it is. The last enemy. I can tell you straight that I do not look forward to death, but I am not frightened by it, because Jesus has defeated it. And no chapter on death, no Christian's reflections, will be complete without thinking on the resurrection. Not just Jesus' resurrection, but ours too.

But to begin with, it might be helpful to consider why death exists in God's world. It exists because God tells the truth, he is not a liar. In the beginning God said to Adam 'On the day you eat of this, that is the day you die.' I take it he said that in the sense that a headmaster might say to a student, 'the day you put graffiti on the wall, that is the day you'll be leaving the school'. If graffiti is discovered, it may not mean the student leaves on that very day, but he has set in motion the series of events that lead ultimately to his expulsion from the school. Now we know that Adam ate the fruit of the knowledge of good and evil, and if Adam had not died, then God would have been a liar. And that would have been a monstrous thing. But God is not a liar. And since we have all sinned and fallen short of the glory of God, we all must die. We all experience the consequences of Adam's sin, and receive the wages for our own.[2]

It was the whole issue of death that persuaded me to become a creationist. If evolution were true then death would have had to have existed before Adam sinned, because the fossil record is a record of dead animals, and some cases, dead people. But the Bible is clear.

> For as by a man came death, by a man
> has come also the resurrection of the
> dead. For as in Adam all die, so also in
> Christ shall all be made alive.
> (1 Corinthians 15:21)

Through Christ all *may* live, but sadly, before that, through Adam all **must** die. And where a baby

---

[2] Of course, if you have been deceived into believing, by faith, Darwin's account of world history, then you will not believe the truth revealed in Genesis. But once we see that the fossil record is the record of a global flood in the time of Noah, and that God made dinosaurs on the sixth day when he made all land animals, we come to realise the Biblical account is much more consistent, sensible and explanatory than any man-made theory. See Answers in Genesis website for more details of the science which confirms the Bible's account of the origin of the species.

dies, and it is difficult to see how he or she could have sinned in the womb, I think we just need to recognise that death comes to us all, because we are Adam's children. David lost his son because of his adultery with Bathsheba and the murder of Uriah, so too Adam has lost his children, some before they were born, because of his sin.

So as we begin thinking about this subject, lets not deceive ourselves into thinking death is something good. It isn't. It is the end result of sin, the payment for sin. Despite this, we probably have known people who looked forward to death — even non-Christians sometimes look forward to dying. And I have found that the reason why some people look forward to death, at the end of a long life, is because they are tired. Death is likened to sleep in the Bible. Just as we look forward to a good night's sleep at the end of a busy day, so people who have lived a long time often look forward to death. However, there is one key difference, I look forward to sleep after a hard day's work only because I expect that I will wake in the morning, and I can only look forward to death armed with the confidence that the Lord will raise me from the dead. If I did not think I was going to get up in the morning I would resist going to bed. If I did not believe in the resurrection of the body, with Jesus the first-fruits, then I would fear death. But as it is, Jesus is risen, he promises to raise all his disciples from the dead - I have confidence in him.

So how does death help the Christian?

Well, generally speaking it doesn't. Jesus came that we might have life in the full, but death stops life. We know that. However, each death we witness reminds us that we need someone to save us — and we have such a saviour in Jesus Christ. Furthermore, each death reminds us that God's word is true. The wages of sin is death, we must be paid our wages.

But also, I think every unrealised dream or hope is a kind of death. When you realise that you're too old to be an All Black, or you'll never own that car you always hoped for, or that you've reached the top of your profession and you'll not go further. In these mini-deaths, which we often call disappointments, we are being pointed towards a much greater death, which is our own. The end of a dream. And the Lord allows all this for a purpose. That we will realise that we cannot live on our own. That every breath we take comes from the Lord, and that eternal life is promised to all who believe in his Son, and look to him, as the Israelites looked to the brass snake in the desert.

Its obvious, I think, to any thinking individual, that death hinders us. It stops us from living forever, it means we can never know our great-grandparents, nor our great-grandchildren. Death creates a sense of urgency in our lives, as we realise there are more books in the world than we could ever read, or places to visit. And when someone we love dies, it hurts terribly. However, we must remember, in the height of great loss, the pain comes from the depth of love we had for the deceased.

The pain we suffer in death is part of the love we enjoy now.

Some people refuse to let go of the dead one — and they put photos up everywhere, and perhaps mark the occasion of the dead person every year with great solemnity. I'm not sure this is helpful. I think God wants us to remember that **he** knows where our loved ones are buried, and that we can be confident he will raise them either to eternal life or judgement. But I think that he wants us, over time, to forget that person, so that new friendships and relationships can form. So the man who loses his father can remember his father with fondness, not with grief, and look to God as his eternal father. The woman who has lost her husband, or the man his wife, can remember what great times they had together, and the memory is clearer as the grief slowly goes.

I've known people to effectively create ghosts, and worship their ancestors, because they failed to let the deceased person go. I knew a woman, I buried her in fact, who became an alcoholic because her 10 month old son had died tragically — she thought she had killed him. But I think the drinking was her mechanism to remember him, rather than to commit him to God for safe-keeping.

The point is, death can hinder us. But the Christian hope is the certain expectation of resurrection to life. The hope a Christian has is that, having died with Christ in this life, he will raise us to life in the age to come. And I thought it would be helpful to consider this hope we have (or can have), in light of those verses in Matthew's gospel that we read and wonder about, but perhaps never quite know what to make of them.

> And behold, the curtain of the temple was torn in two, from top to bottom. And the earth shook, and the rocks were split. The tombs also were opened. And many bodies of the saints who had fallen asleep were raised, and coming out of the tombs after his resurrection they went into the holy city and appeared to many. When the centurion and those who were with him, keeping watch over Jesus, saw the earthquake and what took place, they were filled with awe and said, "Truly this was the Son of God." (Matthew 27:51-54)

We have a strange number of occurrences here. The temple curtain was torn in two, from top to bottom. There was a terrible earthquake which split rocks, tombs were laid open and apparently exposed the bodies. The centurion recognised that Jesus was truly God's son. But the most curious thing, to my mind, is that after Jesus was raised on Resurrection Sunday, many of the saints were raised to eternal life and they came out of their tombs and appeared to people in the city.

The significance of this has been overlooked I think. The simple fact is that Jesus was not the only person raised on that Sunday morning. God raised others. And that raises questions of its own. Were they raised with immortal bodies like Jesus, or simply revived, reconstituted bodies like Lazarus and the little 12 year-old girl?

Did they ascend into heaven, or did they return to their graves? And how old were these saints? Had they been dead for months, years, decades or centuries?

I have been thinking about this because it is one of the most amazing things recorded in history. That one man walked out of his grave, and ascended into heaven, and he is coming again. But not only that, on the day he was raised, others were raised too.

Just think, if you can for a minute, the home town where you grew up. Now imagine that the events of Resurrection Sunday had happened there. In my minds eye I can imagine how shocked I would be to see my grandfather walking down the street. I have a photo of him with my grandmother, I think it may have been their wedding day. There's granddad thirty years old — how would I feel if I saw him walking down the street, and saying hello to me. Then I think of my father's grandfather, my great-grandfather, whom I never knew. What would I say if my father said to me — 'look at that man there Ian, that's your great-grandfather, its granddad — hello granddad!' Can you imagine this? In your mind's eye, your hometown, what it would be like if the dead were raised?

Linda and I walked around the village of Cookham once. Its in Berkshire and a famous artist called Stanley Spencer lived there. Now Spencer painted a picture called resurrection in Cookham churchyard, in which he showed the townspeople getting out of their graves on that last great day when Jesus returns. I commend it to you. But can we imagine what that day will be like? I look forward to it so much!

And the thing this resurrection shows us is that God has set a day on which he will raise the dead and, indeed, judge the world. This resurrection of the saints on Resurrection Sunday was a foretaste of the great resurrection to come. And the Jewish leaders must have been astounded on that day when not only did they hear reports that Jesus had been raised, but that other people were alive too. Who were these saints — we are not told. But perhaps Simeon and Anna, who were there at Jesus' dedication. Perhaps Zechariah and Elizabeth. We simply don't know. I put forward the following thoughts tentatively. I doubt that those raised on that particular Sunday were more than two generations from the generation that was then living.

If my great-grandfather had been raised from the dead, it would have meant nothing to me if I saw him in the street, because I've no idea what he looked like. However, his resurrection would have meant something to my father. It's likely, since the saints made themselves known to those still living, that they must have been known to them before they died. So I suspect it was simply those from one or two generations previous.

Did they ascend to heaven with Jesus? Probably not, because we are told in Hebrews 11 that the saints of old did not receive the promises because they weren't to receive them apart from us. Was King David amongst those raised from the dead? He was surely an Old testament saint of God. But I doubt he was, nobody would have recognised him, because he lived 1000 years before Jesus, and we are told in Acts 2 by Peter:

> "Brothers, I may say to you with confidence about the patriarch David that he both died and was buried, and his tomb is with us to this day. Being therefore a prophet, and knowing that God had sworn with an oath to him that he would set one of his descendants on his throne, he foresaw and spoke about the resurrection of the Christ, that he was not abandoned to Hades, nor did his flesh see corruption. This Jesus God raised up, and of that we all are witnesses. Being therefore exalted at the right hand of God, and having received from the Father the promise of the Holy Spirit, he has poured out this that you yourselves are seeing and hearing. For David did not ascend into the heavens, but he himself says,

> "'The Lord said to my Lord,
> "Sit at my right hand,
> until I make your enemies your
> footstool."
> (Acts 2:29-35)

King David destroyed many enemies of God's people, but he was never powerful enough to conquer death. But his descendent, Jesus of Nazareth, defeated death forever.

Let us consider then the ministry of Jesus with respect to dealing with the dead. Firstly, he raised a twelve year-old girl from the dead. She had only been dead a few minutes, but he went in to the room where she was, with her parents, and James, John and Peter and said 'Talitha kum', little girl, get up — and she did so.

Then, when near the village of Nain, he saw the only son of a widow being carried out in a coffin. The boy had been dead for some hours, we imagine, since the funeral had been organised. Perhaps he had been dead 24 hours, we don't know. Still, Jesus raised him from the dead and restored him to his mother. That was the second resurrection he did.

Then, we read of him raising Lazarus to life. Lazarus had been in the grave for four days when Jesus restored him to life. By that stage, decay would have set in, and a bad smell arising — yet our Lord restored him to perfect health and fulness of life.

So then, we come to Resurrection Sunday, and Jesus is raised from the dead with an immortal, yet touchable body. And with him were raised many saints. God had raised his son from the dead, and a number of saints as well. Now how long had they been dead? Not a few minutes, not a few hours, not a few days, but years, decades even.

Can we even grasp the significance of this? How amazing it must have been in Jerusalem over those few days. And then the news started to spread and it came here, and we have believed it. That one of those who left the grave never returned to it again. A Jewish man by the name of Yeshua, Jesus, had conquered death forever. This helps his disciples so much, for it shows us that the coffin is not an exit-less box, it is a temporary resting place for the saints of God.

Three things for us to consider and apply to our lives then.

Firstly, God was busy that Sunday morning. Anybody who does not believe in God has to explain how it was that those people came back to life. If you accept the account to be true, then it must be the case that God exists, because only he could restore people to life. Someone might say 'well I believe the tomb was emptied, but I don't believe Jesus was raised, the disciples took his body.' Well, on that logic, are we to think that loads of relatives, or perhaps the disciples went down to all these other graves and took out corpses? It defies credibility. If we accept the Bible record to be true, then we know that God exists, and he raises the dead.

Secondly, the resurrection shows us that death has been finally conquered. Death is a battle we will always lose. We may win one round, we may cheat it once or twice, we may postpone it, but we cannot conquer it. But death was not the end for Jesus and it was not, and is not, the end for the saints either. 'What then shall separate us from the love of God, not life, not death, nor anything…'

Thirdly, our future life includes our bodies. They weren't ghosts who walked out of the tombs that day —

anyone could see the tomb was empty. Jesus was at pains to show his disciples he was not a ghost. 'Touch me, you chaps' he says. Look, feel me. 'A ghost doesn't have flesh and bones. I don't suppose you've got anything to eat, have you? I haven't eaten for days.' So they gave him some fish and he ate it.

Do you see? Eternal life means having eternal bodies, with all blemishes removed. I should think that we will look about the same as we did when we were thirty-three, or thereabouts. Spiritualists and mediums believe in ghosts and contacting the spirits, but our expectation is that this earthly tent will be changed into a heavenly one. That our bodies will be raised from the dead. That instead of being clockwork trains that run down, we will be electric trains that run forever, if I can put it that way.

Life shows us death, but it shows us resurrection too. A seed dies, and grows into something better and greater. Physical, but different. What happened to those saints in Jerusalem will happen to every saint on the same day. We'll arrive together, the dead will be raised and then those who still live at his coming will be raised with them.

However, the account in Matthew tells us it was the saints came out of the tombs — those who looked to the Lord. It was not every grave that was emptied in Jerusalem, but the saints only. On resurrection day, the saints will come out. But what about unrepentant sinners?

Lets listen to the clear testimony of scripture.

And many of those who sleep in the dust of the earth shall awake, some to everlasting life, and some to shame and everlasting contempt. And those who are wise shall shine like the brightness of the sky above; and those who turn many to righteousness, like the stars forever and ever. (Daniel 12:2-3)

"Truly, truly, I say to you, an hour is coming, and is now here, when the dead will hear the voice of the Son of God, and those who hear will live. For as the Father has life in himself, so he has granted the Son also to have life in himself. And he has given him authority to execute judgment, because he is the Son of Man. Do not marvel at this, for an hour is coming when all who are in the tombs will hear his voice and come out, those who have done good to the resurrection of life, and those who have done evil to the resurrection of judgment." (John 5:25-29)

Then I saw a great white throne and him who was seated on it. From his presence earth and sky fled away, and no place was found for them. And I saw the dead, great and small, standing before the throne, and books were opened. Then another book was opened, which is the book of life. And the dead were judged by what was written in the books, according to what they had done. And the sea gave up the dead who were in it, Death and Hades gave up the dead who were in them, and they were judged, each one of them, according to what they had done. Then Death and Hades were thrown into the lake of fire. This is the second death, the lake of fire. And if anyone's name was not found written in the book of life, he was thrown into the lake of fire. (Revelation 20:11-15)

Clearly death is not an escape for the sinner.

Now if it were not for the Lord Jesus Christ, I would be terrified of death. But because of him, I do not have to worry, and neither does anyone who is his disciple. Is the Lord Jesus going to leave his brothers and sisters in the tomb? Heaven forbid — but let us then make sure we are his brothers and sisters. Then we need not worry or fear death.

Jesus says 'don't be afraid, I am the first and the last, and the living one; I died, and behold I am alive for evermore, and I have the keys of Death and the grave.'

Death is an enemy conquered.

Death is nightfall, it is eventide.

But every Christian can die saying with confidence 'I'll see you in the morning.'[3]

Lets pray together, lets pray.

---

[3] Indeed, I would like this scripture on my headstone. 'As for me, I shall behold your face in righteousness; when I awake, I shall be satisfied with your likeness.' (Psalm 17:15)

On Banks (and treasures on earth)…

"If a man gives to his neighbour money or goods to keep safe, and it is stolen from the man's house, then, if the thief is found, he shall pay double. If the thief is not found, the owner of the house shall come near to God to show whether or not he has put his hand to his neighbour's property. For every breach of trust, whether it is for an ox, for a donkey, for a sheep, for a cloak, or for any kind of lost thing, of which one says, 'This is it,' the case of both parties shall come before God. The one whom God condemns shall pay double to his neighbour."

(Exodus 22:7-9)

"Do not lay up for yourselves treasures on earth, where moth and rust destroy and where thieves break in and steal, but lay up for yourselves treasures in heaven, where neither moth nor rust destroys and where thieves do not break in and steal. For where your treasure is, there your heart will be also."

(Matthew 8:19-21)

Where do you keep your savings? In a bank or in a tin at home somewhere? If you keep your money in a bank, as most Westerners do, have you thought about why you do that? Is the bank more secure than your own home? Have you ever been burgled?

I presume there are two reasons why we typically use banks. The first is a matter of security. We assume that if cash is stolen from the bank, it will be returned via the insurance company. The second is that the bank will pay interest on the money we lend them (commonly called savings). Money stashed under the sofa, while perhaps not any less secure than deposits in the bank, will not give us any income in the form of interest.

But is this a bad thing? I mentioned in my chapters on money that the whole matter of lending money at interest has become a matter of concern for me. Surely it would be better to lend money privately to family members, or trusted friends, at 0% interest and so bless them.

However, the obvious problem here is that money loses its value. If I lend £5000.00 to someone today, that money will not buy as much five years from now as it will today. This raises the question 'why does money lose value?' Is it possible that the bankers to whom we lend money, or the governments who tax us, cause the money to lose value? And if that's the case, is there anyway to stop your savings losing its value, while at the same time not storing up treasures on earth?

Well, it turns out the reason money loses value is because there is not a fixed amount of British pounds (or US dollars) in circulation. Any time we hear the phrase 'Quantitive Easing' what we are being told is that money is being produced out of nothing and placed in the money system. As more money enters a particular country, its value decreases (because there is more of it). Typically this is called inflation. The government (or bank) is inflating the amount of money in circulation. Money doesn't come into existence by itself, inflation doesn't happen by itself. There is always an agent causing it.

Perhaps an illustration will help. In a certain village there were 100 gold coins. The villagers decided to have one man guard their coins, and he gave them receipts for the coins they had deposited. Realising that it was unlikely that all villagers would approach him at the same time for their money, he began to lend out their money at interest. But instead of giving the coins, he again gave out paper receipts. After a while, the man saw that this was a way for him to make money, so he began to give out receipts for coins that he did not even have. Soon there were 200 receipts in the village, although there were only 100 coins lodged with him. This meant that as long as the villagers did not all come to the bank at the same time for their coins, the village economy could keep running.

However, there was an unforeseen side-effect. Because there were more receipts in the village, but the number of loaves of bread, cheeses and other goods were relatively the same number as before, the prices for these products rose. Whereas before a loaf of bread cost a quarter of a coin, now it cost half a coin. The same thing happened with milk. And so on.

This situation carried on for a long time, until one day a number of villagers decided they wanted to move to another village and to take their money with them. The receipts would be no good to them in the new village, but when they went to the bank with their receipts to collect their gold coins, they found that there weren't enough coins for them all. The bank collapsed and many people lost money, including the original investors.

The situation could have been avoided if the banker had not given out receipts for coins which he did not have. The consequence of this was an increase in prices in the village for many years, and many people losing their money. A better operation would have been for the banker to only lend out a small percentage of the coins, and fixing the currency to the true number of gold coins that there actually were in the village.

The economy described in the village is exactly the kind of economy that most western countries now operate. Many years ago Great Britain and the United States of America went off the gold standard. To give you an idea of how money has lost value, in 1987 an ounce of gold cost £100.00. In 2015 it cost £800.00. It is not true to say that gold has increased in value, rather, the truth is that the British pound is now only worth one-eighth of what it was.

It is for this reason (the constant introduction of money into the system) that house prices keep rising. It's not that your house is worth more, but that money is worth less. The older a house is, in many ways, the less valuable it is, because it will need more maintenance. Similarly, it is for this reason a 100 page paperback book in 1985 cost only 95 pence, while in 2015 it cost £4.99.

It is completely impossible to stop your money from losing its value, because governments and banks actively work to introduce money into their respective monetary systems. Even if you were to withdraw all your cash today from the bank, while you might save yourself from a later run on the bank should their tactics become widely known, your money will still lose its purchasing power.

The solution to this seems to me to buy things of a fixed quantity. Gold and property are the obvious examples. If you know that it will cost you £9000.00 to send your child to university, rather than try and save the money when they're young, it would be better to buy gold. When you have the equivalent of £9000.00 in gold in today's currency, you no longer need to buy any more. Even if your child is just two years old, you can reasonably expect that the gold you buy today will be worth whatever the cost of university education is 16 years hence. However, if you stick with the traditional method of depositing money in the bank you can never be sure if the figure in the bank will be enough in 16 years time.

From a Biblical perspective I see it this way. God made gold (it's an element in the periodic table) as well as silver, as well as land. But paper money is a man-made invention, and so will never be as good as something the Lord made. In addition, because Western men are typically driven by money and wealth (unrighteous mammon) we can be pretty sure that bankers will do what they can to make money, without fully considering the moral consequences. This means that money in banks will always be insecure, prone to theft, and forever losing value.

All of which goes to show that really, if we are Christians, we ought to have our treasure in heaven. For where our treasure is, there our hearts will be. Jesus does not say 'where your heart is, there your treasure will be.' No, he shows us that our hearts follow our treasure. Lets store up treasure in heaven by obeying the king of the kingdom of heaven. All money carries risk in this life, its far better to trust in the God and Father of our Lord Jesus Christ, asking him for our daily bread…

Give us today our daily bread, and lead us not into temptation,
for thine is the kingdom, the power, and the glory, forever and ever,
Amen.

On Disappointments...

The Christian Life certainly has its helps, it has its hindrances, its hopes and its fears. We all know that disappointments are a part of the life. But what are they? It's good to remember disappointments are simply unrealised hopes. That's all they are.

Three things generally cause disappointments. Situations. People. God. We might as well face it that sometimes Christians feel disappointed by God, generally when our prayers are not answered. The classic Biblical example is Jonah. He was disappointed the Lord did not destroy Nineveh. Was Jonah's attitude right? No. But he demonstrates human thinking. We do have expectations of the Lord. Here are some people who had their share of disappointments, as recorded in the Bible:

1 Samuel 8:1-7 - Samuel was disappointed in his sons.

He was disappointed by the people.

He'd worked hard at his job, served the Lord, and they did not want him nor his family to continue. In 1 Samuel 15:34-35 we learn that Samuel was disappointed by Saul, the one the Lord had told him should be king. But note it, the Lord himself was disappointed in Saul.

Our Lord Jesus appears to have been disappointed by the disciples slowness to learn. He had to rebuke Peter at one point, and on the night of his betrayal he says 'have I been with you so long Phillip and yet you do not know me? He who has seen me has seen the father.'

In addition, it appears the Lord was disappointed by mankind in the time of Noah. We can read about this in Genesis 6.6 It's a good lesson to learn that we can cause the Lord disappointments, or, to put it another way, we can disappoint the Lord. Yes, we can let him down.

Helps - the Lord wants us to learn from our dashed hopes. Firstly, that all human sources of hope and expectation will, at some point, fail. For instance, a congregation may have high hopes of their pastor, but it is inevitable that he will disappoint you at some time. This might be because the hopes are unrealistic or misplaced, or that the thing it is hoped the pastor will do is beyond his power.

We may have hopes for our children, and yet inevitably they will disappoint us at some point, just as the children may hope something of their parents, but are disappointed by them. A relative of mine had asked his father for a toy gun for his birthday. The lad's father bought him a bow and arrow instead. The boy was exceedingly disappointed by his father, and spoke often of this incident, well into his adulthood. But we must learn a lesson from disappointment - firstly, that the only source of true satisfaction will be found in the Lord.

And when he disappoints us, when we feel he hasn't answered our prayers, we can be sure that the problem lies in what we hoped and prayed for, and probably in our misunderstanding of what love truly is, and what the Lord's purposes are. Because God always knows the best outcome, and gives us opportunities for learning. I know a couple who were married a number of years ago. On the honeymoon, it looked like the wife had fallen pregnant. Her monthly cycle was delayed, first a week late, then two, and she and her husband thought — maybe we're expecting a baby. But then, it came to pass that obviously she was not pregnant. Whether the baby was lost, or whether it had never actually been conceived they do not know — but they were disappointed. However, they learnt a valuable lesson. That it is foolish to think you can just have children when you want, because Scripture says it is the Lord who opens and closes the womb. So they changed their whole approach from thinking we'll have child A in this year, and child B in this year, instead they put the whole matter in the Lord's hands and received children when he gave them. In this way their disappointment helped them, for they learnt a lesson from it.

Secondly, a disappointment can help us by spurring us on to a new thing that we would never have looked for, had we not been disappointed first. I failed my last semester at Bible College. I was bitterly disappointed, but it was because of that failure that I took up doing a Master's degree at Exeter University. I was greatly helped by doing that degree, in some senses what I learnt shaped my preaching. It certainly shaped my thinking. But it would not have happened, but for the earlier disappointment.

85

Hindrances

Sometimes people hope and pray for things, and its right we do so, because only the Lord can help us with our request. But what if the answer comes back as 'no' - 'no, I have plans for you that you don't know yet. But that thing you are hoping for will not come to pass. Yet, will you still follow me?' This was the case with C.S. Lewis. He prayed his mother might live, but she didn't. So his faith was hindered by the unanswered prayer.

We may think, prayer doesn't work. But the truth is, it's not prayer that doesn't work, it's simply that God quite often says no. Those of us with children will know how often we say no to our children, yet it does not mean we don't love them. We need to be aware that unanswered prayers can hinder us, because the thing we want is very precious to us. But it seems to me that the Lord deliberately doesn't respond to our petitions on many occasions, and this might be because he's teaching us to trust him, or he's testing our faith to see if we'll stay close to him even in adversity (because he does not want fair-weather friends), or even because he's disciplining us, because we have not yet learnt a valuable lesson.

Unanswered prayers are often disappointing. Sometimes though, we are grateful, in hindsight, that prayers have not been answered. And it is certainly true that unanswered prayers and various disappointments in life can do one thing that answered prayers can never do. They give us an opportunity to show God we will trust him even in disappointment.

<u>Hopes</u>

What might we hope for, in the face of disappointments? How do we overcome the disappointment of a lost friendship, or relationship, or an unrealised goal? Looking at the big picture - Firstly, lets remember our purpose in life is to bring glory to God, not for some other reason. It is easy to take the good gifts that God has given us, and accidentally turn them into idols. A good wife is from the Lord, but it's not difficult for a man to start living for his wife instead of for God. It's worth thinking carefully about how we glorify him amidst disappointments.

Has God allowed a disappointment to happen because we have wandered off the path and started desiring something more than we should do? Often the thing we hope for, we want, is because we feel it will give us some status and some identity. When I was a teenager I failed to make the First XV rugby squad. I was very disappointed. But why did I want to be in the team? It was for the prestige. If someone had come alongside me and said 'you know what Ian, it doesn't matter that you're not in the team. God still values you and is looking out for you, and it must be the case he has other plans for you — that is why you've not made the team this year' that would have been a big help. When we live for God's glory, then our disappointments can be used for him. Because its in adversity that our real commitment to God is made clear. One of Israel's prophets shows us this:

> Though the fig tree should not blossom,
> nor fruit be on the vines,
> the produce of the olive fail
> and the fields yield no food,
> the flock be cut off from the fold
> and there be no herd in the stalls,
> yet I will rejoice in the Lord;
> I will take joy in the God of my salvation.
> (Habakkuk 3.17)

Habakkuk says he will rejoice in the Lord no matter what. Habakkuk sees the big picture. He lives for God's glory. And that is, I think, one of the hopes God has for us, when we experience a disappointment.

Secondly, lets remember that God disciplines his children, and no discipline seems pleasant at the time, but later it produces a harvest of righteousness. In hindsight we can see God working for our good where at the time we did not understand. The lesson is that we are a work of art in God's hands. Clay in the master potter's spinning wheel, living stones fashioned by the master creator. Now a work of art may not always be treated kindly, but it is treated lovingly by the artist. The master artist may rub out and restart various times on his life's work, not because he has made a mistake but because the artwork is not yet what he wants it to be. If we were the painting we might rather the artist didn't spend so much time on us, but God is not making a sketch for a child, but a work of art. So we may have to start again — getting rid of sins and idols that have crept in unawares. But its God's hope, or expectation, to make us into the image of Jesus. Clones of Jesus, if you like. And this happens in space and time, and disappointments may well be part of the creative process.

Fears

After the death of our Lord, the disciples were fearful to go out and about. They had been crushed by disappointment. They had hoped that they would enter Jerusalem, and Jesus would set up God's kingdom, and they would reign with him. No more Romans about, no more legalistic religious people. Can you imagine their sadness and disappointment? But then Jesus appeared to them and they realised that their hopes had been in the wrong place. God's plan had been far bigger than throwing the Romans out of Jerusalem - it was his plan to conquer sin and death through his Son.

We may have been disappointed by something in the past, and we may now be fearful of the future. 'I had a good friend once, but she let me down, so I'm not going to get close to anyone again.' 'Yes, I had hoped to do this, I prayed about it, but the Lord did not bring it to pass. So, I'm giving up on prayer and, I realise now that God has few plans for me.'

That's not the way God wants us to live. The world is not impressed by Christians who don't take any risks for the Lord. The world is impressed by Christians who show the world that God is more important to us than anything else, so that we risk disappointment. Esther overcame the disappointment of her parents death and then leaving her uncle's house, to enter the king's palace. She overcame her fear and risked her life to speak to the king, even though it was illegal.

Shadrach, Meshach, Abednego overcame the disappointment of Jerusalem being captured and their being relocated to Babylon. But they lived by faith, telling the king they would not bow down to his idol. Paul overcame his disappointments and lived by faith, and so he was useful in the Lord's service. He showed the world that knowing Jesus Christ was more important to him than anything else. He was faithful unto death.

The point is, how we handle loss and disappointment shows the world who our treasure is. The world is not impressed when Christians get rich and say thanks to God. They are impressed when God is so satisfying that we give our riches away for Christ's sake and count it gain. We must not fear living life and perhaps taking risks for the Lord, for fear of disappointment. Shall I tell you one of my biggest fears, something that will really disappoint me as a pastor? I will be disappointed if, in the course of my ministry, I am unable to persuade you to live for Jesus and not to waste your life. I know a man who worked hard and dreamed of a happy retirement with his wife. Then she contracted ME and their dreams of a happy retirement were shattered, she was too weak to do anything really. But what's sad is not that she got ME, but that he thought that waiting until retirement was the right thing to do, before he started living. Jesus calls us to live now. That's why I get cross with the amount of time Christians spend watching TV, or messing around on Facebook. At the end of time, do you want to say to the Lord 'look Lord, how I spent the time you gave me. 30,000 hours of watching TV.' Does it not seem to us a waste of life to spend hours looking at flickering images that we cannot remember the next day? Doesn't it seem to you that Jesus is calling us to a higher life?

In life we will have disappointments. And God wants us to overcome them. Turn with me to Romans 5 as we close:

> Therefore, since we have been justified by faith, we have peace with God through our Lord Jesus Christ. Through him we have also obtained access by faith into this grace in which we stand, and we rejoice in hope of the glory of God. Not only that, but we rejoice in our sufferings, knowing that suffering produces endurance, and endurance produces character, and character produces hope, and hope does not put us to shame, because God's love has been poured into our hearts through the Holy Spirit who has been given to us.

Disappointments are simply unrealised hopes. That's all they are. Disappointments produce endurance, and endurance produces character, and character produces hope. And we are to hope in the glory of God. Not that our children might become brain surgeons, nor that we might become CEOs, but in the glory of God.

That God might be the most important thing in our lives.

In the resurrection of Jesus we see God conquering disappointment. Whatever disappointments we feel now, or will feel this week, lets not lose sight of the fact that Jesus comes to his disciples and says 'do you love me, more than all these other things? Then come, I have work for you to do.' Don't let fear of failure stop us from living for the Lord. Don't let it stop you from writing the book you always wanted to write. Don't let it stop you from having the child you always wanted. Don't let disappointments stop us from living. Disappointments are part of life itself.

Applications:

Has someone disappointed you? Remember, you will probably also have disappointed that person at some point. Forgiveness is key. Have you been disappointed by an unrealised goal? Take comfort that the Lord brings good out of bad, and that when one door is closed it can well be because he is going to open another one. King David was disappointed not to make a house for the Lord, but the Lord planned to make a house for him.

In my own life, I was disappointed because I wanted to go to Bible College in Oxford, but was turned down. That was God's plan, for I was to meet Linda in North London at college, which would never have happened had I gone to Oxford.

Have you felt disappointed by the Lord? Remember, you will probably have disappointed him at some point too. And remember this, that God's pure and perfect love, is not simply kindness. Kindness is an aspect of love, but does not capture all of what love means. I would not think much of a friend who said to me he didn't care if I was dishonest, or cheating on my wife, provided I was happy. And God's love for us is not kindness in the sense that all he cares about is our happiness, rather his love for us is such that he will step in, if we are idolising things we should not, or walking a path that is not good for us. Because we are a work of art.

God does not exist to make us happy, it would be closer to the truth to see it the other way around. We exist to make him happy, or even more accurately, to bring him glory. Lets look at John's gospel to close. John 21:18

> "Truly, truly, I say to you, when you were young, you used to dress yourself and walk wherever you wanted, but when you are old, you will stretch out your hands, and another will dress you and carry you where you do not want to go." (This he said to show by what kind of death he was to glorify God.) And after saying this he said to him, "Follow me"

Was Peter disappointed to hear how he was going to die? We don't know. But his death was to glorify God, just as his life was. You and I may be disappointed in life, but we were created to bring glory to God. And often it will be in the midst of disappointments that we will glorify him the best. Our Lord Jesus' words to Peter are the same to us. "Follow me." The Lord of glory simply says, 'follow me.'

A Prayer for the disappointed:

Lord, we recognise that in a fallen world we will often be disappointed. Help us to see that hopes often are unrealised because you have a greater plan than we, with limited understanding, can see. Forgive us our many sins Lord, and please would you move the hearts of those whom we have disappointed, to forgive us, just as we forgive those who have disappointed us. And Lord, please forgive us where we have felt disappointed by you. The truth is that we must have disappointed you many more times and in many different ways, without even knowing it. Thank you that your love for us means that you will, from time to time, disappoint us. Sometimes you will take our idols from us, because we will not give them up or see them in the right light. But above all Lord, we thank you that your son never disappointed you. And even though he suffered, he never lost faith in you, and you delivered him from death.

Help us to rejoice in our sufferings o Lord, knowing that suffering produces endurance, and endurance produces character, and ultimately, character produces a hope that does not disappoint us or put us to shame, because your love has been poured into our hearts through the Holy Spirit whom you have given to us. We ask this in Jesus' name, Amen.

On Rest...

Earlier in this book I suggested some ways in which work fits into the Christian's life. We saw that work helps us by making us a little like God, because God worked in the beginning and works now. We saw that work hinders us, because the world is fallen, so that sin makes work unpleasant because of the laziness of ourselves, or our colleagues; or it makes us spend too much time away from other things that have a legitimate claim on our time. In short, work can become an idol. We saw that one of the expectations or hopes that God has for us is that we should redeem our work places, making them better than they ever were. Perhaps the workplace is our greatest opportunity to obey Jesus when he says… 'Let your light shine before others, so that they may see your good works and give glory to your Father who is in heaven.'

Then we saw that one of the great fears people have is that their work will be wasted. That after we die, or move away, all that we worked for will be lost forever. And we saw that the only work that has lasting value, is the work that contributes to the eternal kingdom.

> "Do not work for the food that perishes, but for the food that endures to eternal life, which the Son of Man will give to you. For on him God the Father has set his seal." Then they said to him, "What must we do, to be doing the works of God?" Jesus answered

them, "This is the work of God, that you believe in him whom he has sent."

So we come to the 'flip-side' of work, which is rest. How does rest help us in the Christian life? Can it hinder us from growing as Christians - if so, how? What hopes should we have, as disciples of Jesus, of rest; and what things about rest might cause us fear? This may sound far-fetched, but we've probably known times when we have been anxious about going on holiday. Anxiety is simply a form of fear, so what things are there about rest which we might find fearful, and are there any warnings in scripture that we should heed?

So it's the Christian life, looking at rest, and beginning with how rest helps us.

A question to begin. Does God want us to rest?

Well, its obvious from reading Scripture that God is concerned about his people finding rest. Hence Genesis 2.

> Thus the heavens and the earth were finished, and all the host of them. And on the seventh day God finished his work that he had done, and he rested on the seventh day from all his work that he had done. So God blessed the seventh day and made it holy, because on it God rested from all his work that he had done in creation.

The Sabbath was created by God for man's benefit, not because God was tired - but because man is made in God's image. God wanted to enjoy all that he has created, and he wants us to enjoy the fruit of our work too. And we cannot enjoy the labour of our hands if we are forever labouring.

On day six God made Adam and Eve, and he enjoyed their company on the seventh day — the first Sabbath day was spent with Adam and Eve together, after Adam had worked the day before, naming the animals.

Humans are made in the image of God, a God who works, but who *does not always work*. He took time out in the beginning to enjoy the fruits of his labours, and so should we. Now-a-days we live in a world that says we ought to rest two days a week, and we ought only work 40 hours a week. But this isn't God's pattern. I have found that by trusting God, and mentally throwing the 40-hour week out the window, my rest and my work times have greatly improved. God's word does not say 'work only 40 hours a week,' God says 'work six days a week, and rest on the seventh.' So changing my attitude from that of the world's, to that of God's, helps free me from feelings of exploitation if I do work more than 40 hours a week. Do you see what I mean here? If you think you should only work forty hours a week, and your boss or your job requires you to do more, then you will feel hard-done by. But if you see that God calls us to work six days a week, then it won't be a problem for us to do so. And then our rest days will be all the more meaningful.

Rest is a blessing from God. But we ought not just wait until the seventh day to get our rest, we ought also to have proper rest every day. We receive this in the form of sleep.

> In peace I will both lie down and sleep;
> for you alone, O Lord, make me dwell in safety.
> Psalm 4:8

Maybe the chief enemy of a good sleep is anxiety. We can take a day off a week, but we will not get rest from it if we are anxious. No doubt this is why Jesus commands us - and it is a command - not to worry. If we worry about tomorrow, we are saying in our hearts 'whatever comes along tomorrow Lord, I don't believe you can handle it.' This is a wicked thing for a Christian to think. 'There are things out there too big for you to handle dad' is the lie that hides behind worrying or fretting. It is a sin, because when we worry we are disobeying a command of Jesus. And all that worry does, is steal our rest. But God's intention is that we should rest at the end of a long day — not to be like a farmer who spent all day turning over his fields and then at night, turning things over in his mind.

If we are in the habit of worrying, or if unusual events are causing us distress, there is something we must remember, and something we must do. The thing we must remember is that 'perfect love casts out all fear.' Anxiety is caused by fearing the loss of something. Suppose, for instance, you are fearful of losing your job or perhaps a loved one, or even life itself. If we remember that every good gift comes to us from God, the Father of lights, and that we are to love the giver more than the gift, then our love for the Lord will help us conquer the fear. If I fear that I will lose my job, and I worry about it, then I am loving the job more than I am loving God, who gave it to me. For it may be God's will that I lose the job, in order to make me grow, or become more like his Son. So we must remember that perfect love casts out all fear. That our prayer should be 'Father, if it be thy will, take this cup from me - nevertheless, not my will but thine be done.'

So the thing to remember is perfect love casts out fear. The thing to do is to get on our knees and pray. We may need to confess our sin first, ask for forgiveness, and give the issue over to God. And if that worry creeps back into your mind, pray again. 'Father, if it be thy will, take this cup from me — nevertheless, not my will but thine be done.'

I was at school years ago as an exchange student with the cousin of John Cougar Mellencamp - an American pop singer. He had a song once with a line in it that said 'I've worried about many things, most of which did not come to pass...' And if we think about the things that have worried us in the past, we will see we only hurt ourselves by worrying, and all we did was lose our sleep and our rest. I do not say avoiding anxiety is easy, quite the opposite. But the point I'm making is that true rest comes from a peaceful mind, not an anxious one.

In peace I will both lie down and sleep;
for you alone, O Lord, make me dwell in safety.

Psalm 4:8

Now if we consider the fourth commandment for a moment we see something else about Sabbath rest is helpful.

> ***Remember*** the Sabbath day, to keep it holy. Six days you shall labor, and do all your work, but the seventh day is a Sabbath to the Lord your God. On it you shall not do any work, you, or your son, or your daughter, your male servant, or your female servant, or your livestock, or the sojourner who is within your gates. For in six days the Lord made heaven and earth, the sea, and all that is in them, and rested on the seventh day. Therefore the Lord blessed the Sabbath day and made it holy.

The commandment calls us to *remember* the Sabbath. That's because there is the constant temptation to forget it. We will not be tempted to remember it, but to forget it. So we need to make an effort to ensure we get the rest the Lord wants us to have. Furthermore, the commandment calls for rest for our servants, that is, any employees we may have, as well as for the livestock we may own. Even animals are entitled to rest too.

It was thinking about this that I stopped turning on my laptop on the Sabbath. I suggest to you that taking your laptop on holiday, or switching it on on your day off, will inevitably lead you into working. You'll get an email you need to respond to, or you'll check your work email to see what is happening. But if we applied God's commandment more accurately to our lives, then our rest would be better.

So the Christian life — rest, how does it help us? It helps us switch off from regular work, it gives us time to be with those whom we love and in some senses work for. It gives us a chance to be with the Lord, and by understanding that God designed us to rest only one day from seven, instead of two days in seven, we will become more productive in our Father's world. In times of extreme busy-ness the Lord Jesus made sure that his disciples got some extra time off. Mark 6.

> The apostles returned to Jesus and told him all that they had done and taught. And he said to them, "Come away by yourselves to a desolate place and rest a while." For many were coming and going, and they had no leisure even to eat. And they went away in the boat to a desolate place by themselves.

Getting away from the regular busy-ness of life is something our Lord did — daily for prayer, it seems, and here, after an exceptionally busy period of work where Jesus and the disciples hardly had time to eat, they went to a desolate place. So rest is a good thing that helps God's people. It is woven into the fabric of creation.

But rest can also be a hindrance in the Christian life. Too many holidays and not enough work will soon mean that the holidays become tiresome, and unfulfilling. Indeed, holidays improperly planned can often lead to greater tiredness after the holiday than before it. Why should that be? Well, as ever, God's word provides us with insight into these matters.

First, holidaying too much, or resting too much, can tempt us to sin. Laziness is a sin. The Lord created us to serve him, to fill the earth with children, to have dominion over his creation. This is why having children is a great blessing, because having them is part of God's plan for mankind. The more children we have, the greater the blessing. Yes, the workload increases, but not in proportion to the increase in the blessing. This is also why having a lawn or garden that is neatly mown and weeded is so much more attractive than an unweeded garden and unmown lawn. Keeping things in order is obeying that first command given to our ancestors, and it explains why we find a tidy lawn so much more a blessing than a messy one.

But if we rest too much, then we get lazy. God's word reminds us 'The sluggard buries his hand in the dish and will not even bring it back to his mouth. The sluggard does not plough in the autumn; he will seek at harvest and have nothing.' Too much rest without proper amount of work may also lead us to become busy-bodies. This can be a temptation whenever we lack the routine that work establishes, and we can poke our noses in where it is not really wanted or needed. Paul warns us about this.

> For even when we were with you, we would give you this command: If anyone is not willing to work, let him not eat. For we hear that some among you walk in idleness, not busy at work, but busybodies. Now such persons we command and encourage in the Lord Jesus Christ to do their work quietly and to earn their own living.

A lust for leisure time and not working may lead us into theft, which is what many people do through benefit fraud. If we take a benefit which we don't truly need or deserve, we are making tax-payers pay for our laziness. Certainly then as Christians we need to be aware of these temptations and resist them if necessary.

Secondly, holidays can hinder us in the Christian life by taking us away from a regular routine, making us tired because all is a state of change, as opposed to a state of order. I am sure all of us have had holidays where we returned home more tired than when we left. Why should this be? Why should a time of supposed rest actually leave us exhausted?

I think part of this has to do with routine. Routine is a form of discipline that helps us run our days in an orderly fashion. So we eat meals at regular times, work at regular times, etc. The discipline helps us because it means we know what we are going to do without needing to exercise much thought - extended thinking and decision making is tiring. When it comes then to holidays, the regular discipline of the day is removed. The change is greater than we can handle, and so we get tired instead of resting.

As a race, mankind desires change, but predictable change. We like the change of seasons, but only so long as they change in a regular order. We would tire of a permanent summer, but we would be exhausted if, at the end of summer, we did not know which season was next coming upon us. We like change but also regular rhythm. Now a holiday will hinder us from proper rest if the regular rhythm is disturbed. In other words, if we normally go to bed at 10.30, staying up to 11.30 will be quite tiring, even if we sleep an extra hour at the other end.

Too much rest can hinder us in the Christian life. Our Lord said that he came not to be served, but to serve, and he who would be great must be the servant of all. If we rest for too long, we will stop serving and start lording it over others. So rest helps us by making us a little bit like God, who rested after his work and enjoyed the fruit of his labours, but rest can hinder us, by making us lazy, or by removing certain routines whose existence discipline us and make us productive.

So we come to hopes. What is God's hope for mankind with respect to rest? What was God's purpose in designing holidays, because we read of a number of them in the Old Testament? Israel was given national holidays which forged the identity of the nation. Passover and the Feast of Unleavened Bread gave them an identity as a people delivered from slavery. Pentecost reminded them of the good laws God had given them at Sinai. The Feast of Trumpets looked forward to the day of God's victory, the day of atonement to the banishment of the evil one, the Feast of Tabernacles to that time when God would fully dwell with man.

Great Britain used to have Christian holidays. Christmas, Easter and Whitsunday. I only ever learnt about Whitsunday holidays from an old railway postcard I found. I did not know that for many years the May bank holiday was called the Whitsun holiday and it fell on the same weekend as Pentecost, (Whitsunday is a synonym of Pentecost). So we used to have Christian holidays, including the closure of shops on Sundays. Sunday observance is not strictly Biblical, but it comes from a Christian tradition.

Now the point of holidays is to help give identity. Nations traditionally have been defined by ethnicity, language, institutions and religion. National holidays are part of those institutions a country has, and if they are coupled to religion, then the holidays reinforce the religious beliefs of the country. So holidays, times of national resting, say something about who we are. Christian holidays point to what God has done, and the removal of them from public life is just part of the nation being slowly washed away, as the United Kingdom moves away from the eternal kingdom of God.

So what is God's purpose in resting and in holidays? For the Christian, they give us identity. But its important then that they give us the right identity. A Christian would not celebrate Islamic or Buddhist holidays, so we ought to think carefully about the holidays we do celebrate. For this reason I'd recommend we think about those days in the Christian calendar that were commanded to the Israelites, to see if they can be helpfully incorporated into the Christian life. So, for example, why should we not celebrate Passover - not as Jews, who rejected the Messiah, but as Christians, who recognise Jesus as our Passover lamb. 'Behold the lamb of God, who takes away the sins of the world.' Christ died that the angel of destruction might passover us, that we might not be destroyed on the day of judgement, that we might leave a land of sin, and follow the true and living God. Why not celebrate that as a passover meal, as Messianic Jews do?

So one of the hopes of God, with respect to our holidays, is that they will teach us of him. It also appears to me that one of the hopes or expectations of Jesus Christ is that people will come to him for true rest. Hence his famous invitation:

> Come to me, all who labor and are heavy laden, and I will give you rest. Take my yoke upon you, and learn from me, for I am gentle and lowly in heart, and you will find rest for your souls. For my yoke is easy, and my burden is light.

God's hope, if I can put it like this, was that the Biblical holidays celebrated by the Israelites would lead them to see that true rest is found in Jesus himself. The holy days are just images of the real thing. We must not mistake the image for the real thing. Resting on a holiday or on the Sabbath is only an image of the rest we find in Christ. It is seeing through the glass darkly, whereas in Christ we find and will find proper and perfect rest.

Let me try and illustrate this a different way. There was a man who was tired of doing things the old way. Nothing seemed to satisfy, he couldn't get no satisfaction. He had a wife, 2.8 children, house, dog and the cat — holidays in Majorca (but sometimes in Scotland). And he thought - "is this it? Why does this life not give me the rest I desire? Whenever I achieve something, it satisfies for only a short time, and then I must chase something different. Will I ever find true and proper rest?" But then he came to Jesus, who said 'Take my yoke upon you and learn from me…'

Then he learnt two things. How he should truly live in a way that satisfied, and the promise of true rest in the age to come.

So the Lord taught him that 2.8 children was the world's idea, not his, for it was the Lord's will that men should marry and go forth and multiply. So that affected his sex life and his attitude towards children. Then he learnt a good father is careful to discipline his child, so that made him pay more attention to training his children rightly, and he eliminated much of the exhaustion they caused by teaching them to be obedient and not to back-chat.

Then he learnt that a man's life does not consist in the abundance of his possessions, so that affected his attitude towards acquiring things. Then he learnt that God wanted him to work for his glory, so he began to see his office as a place of serving the Lord. Then he learnt that the Lord wanted him to stop grumbling about the weather and about politicians, for he saw that the Lord sent the rain on the good and bad alike, and raised up rulers. So he gave up complaining, and he found rest there. And so it went on. That the man who truly came to Jesus found true rest there. Which was God's 'hope' all along.

And so we come, to the promise of eternal rest, which also introduces the subject of fears. There is a land promised to us, but the author of Hebrews raises the fear that we might not reach it. True saints will persevere to the end, but true saints will do so by heeding the warnings. For the warnings are real. So then, lets turn to Hebrews 4.

> Therefore, while the promise of entering his rest still stands, let us fear lest any of you should seem to have failed to reach it. For good news came to us just as to them, but the message they heard did not benefit them, because they were not united by faith with those who listened. For we who have believed enter that rest, as he has said,
>
> > "As I swore in my wrath,

'They shall not enter my rest,'"
although his works were finished from the foundation of the world. For he has somewhere spoken of the seventh day in this way: "And God rested on the seventh day from all his works." And again in this passage he said,

"They shall not enter my rest."
Since therefore it remains for some to enter it, and those who formerly received the good news failed to enter because of disobedience, again he appoints a certain day, "Today," saying through David so long afterward, in the words already quoted,

"Today, if you hear his voice, do not harden your hearts."
For if Joshua had given them rest, God would not have spoken of another day later on. So then, there remains a Sabbath rest for the people of God, for whoever has entered God's rest has also rested from his works as God did from his. Let us therefore strive to enter that rest, so that no one may fall by the same sort of disobedience.

The generation of Israelites that left Egypt, did not enter the promised land because they did not carry on in faith. We are urged as Christians, not to be disbelieving, or lose faith in the one who saved us, but to carry on, striving to enter that rest which God will give to all his children. When we are tired, or struggling in our faith, let us go near the throne of grace that we may receive mercy and grace in our time of need. Let us have faith, so that after 40 or so years of wandering in this life, until we finally fall asleep in death, we can be confident our Lord will lift us up, at the resurrection, into the promised land forever.

To conclude:

Rest helps us in the Christian life by giving us time to enjoy the fruit of our labour and to spend time with God, which would be impossible if we worked all the time.

Our rest can be hindered by anxiety, so we must remember that perfect love casts out fear and that prayer is the antidote to worry. Rest can hinder us if by it we become lazy, or if it is not properly structured and thus a regular daily rhythm is lost.

It was God's hope that Old Testament holidays would provide national identity to the Jews, and this ought to make us, as Christians, reflect on the holidays we will observe. Furthermore, we can hope to find our ultimate rest in obedience to Jesus, because when we do things his way we find ourselves at peace. Finally, we have the sure promise of a rest to come, but the Bible warns us to fear the possibility of not reaching it, which will happen if we do not learn the lessons of the Israelites, who fell by disobedience.

Rest is a blessing from God. But just like any other blessing, we must not mistake it for God himself, and so idolise it, nor must we neglect it, and so fail to gain the wonderful blessings that come from it. Let us not forget that we live in a world that would have us work forever, to keep us permanently away from the Lord God, who alone gives us true rest. Let us therefore strive to enter that rest, so that no one may fall. For the word of God is living and active, sharper than any two-edged sword, piercing to the division of soul and of spirit, of joints and of marrow, and discerning the thoughts and intentions of the heart.

Afterword...

My thoughts stop at this point, but if you have found them helpful, perhaps you could lend this book to someone else. Or better still, buy your friends their own copy. I know I would appreciate it, as would my family, because all proceeds from book sales go towards our ever increasing food bill.

God ever bless you.

I.W.C.

25280923R00072

Printed in Great Britain
by Amazon